South Africa
and Its
Neighbors

A World Peace Foundation Book

South Africa and Its Neighbors

Regional Security and Self-Interest

Robert I. Rotberg
Massachusetts Institute of Technology

Henry S. Bienen
Princeton University

Robert Legvold
Columbia University

Gavin G. Maasdorp
University of Natal

Lexington Books
D.C. Heath and Company/Lexington, Massachusetts/Toronto

Library of Congress Cataloging in Publication Data
Main entry under title:

South Africa and its neighbors.

  Bibliography: p.
  Includes index.
  1. South Africa—National security. 2. Africa,
Southern—National security. 3. South Africa—Military
relations—Africa, Southern. 4. Africa, Southern—
Military relations—South Africa. I. Rotberg,
Robert I.

86-7359

UA856.S667   1985   355'.033068   84–48006
ISBN 0–669–09025–5 (alk. paper)

Published simultaneously in Canada
Printed in the United States of America on acid-free paper
International Standard Book Number: 0–669–09025–5
Library of Congress Catalog Card Number: 84–48006

Contents

Preface

This book grew out of "South Africa and Its Neighbors: Policy Questions for the 1980s," a conference sponsored by the World Peace Foundation of Boston and the South African Institute of International Affairs in Johannesburg and held in Natal in early 1984. Robert I. Rotberg of the foundation and John Barratt, director of the institute, chaired the meeting, which was attended by forty Americans, South Africans, and Zimbabweans. The participants included members of the U.S. Senate and the South African Parliament, former ambassadors, judges and other officials, academics, corporate executives, and newspaper editors.

Earlier versions of the chapters that follow by Henry S. Bienen, Robert Legvold, and Gavin G. Maasdorp were among the papers discussed at the conference. Maasdorp's paper formed a part of his *SADCC: A Post-Nkomati Evaluation* (Johannesburg, 1984). His chapter in this book is a revised, updated, and condensed version of that publication, which was issued by the South African Institute of International Affairs. "Decision Making and the Military in South Africa," by Robert I. Rotberg, draws upon an earlier version called "The Process of Decision-Making in Contemporary South Africa," *CSIS Africa Notes*, 22 (28 December 1983). His chapter on "South Africa and the Soviet Union" was first aired in a different format at a meeting at Kent State University in April 1984. His "Namibia" chapter draws for some of its prose on "Namibia and the Crisis of Constructive Engagement," which will appear in James Coleman and Richard Sklar (eds.), *African Crisis Areas and U.S. Foreign Policy* (Berkeley, 1985). Parts of the concluding chapter were initially discussed in a series of meetings in Washington, D.C., and Durham, N.H., in late 1984.

The authors gratefully acknowledge the intelligent criticisms of Richard H. Ullman and the administrative assistance of Pamela W. Smith and Ambassador Richard Bloomfield and the staff of the World Peace Foundation. The index was prepared by Stephanie D. Jones.

—R.I.R., H.S.B., R.L., G.G.M

1

Introduction: South Africa in Its Region—Hegemony and Vulnerability

Robert I. Rotberg

S outh Africa's position as the dominant power in all of southern Africa increased dramatically during the 1980s. By mid-decade, South Africa had no local or global rivals for preeminence in the region south of Zaire and Tanzania. Despite its own profoundly unstable core, the extent of its newly accomplished hegemony had exceeded even the expectations of South Africa's most optimistic strategic planners. Mozambique and Swaziland had become client states in all but name, Botswana and Lesotho had lost much of their previous freedom to pursue thoroughly differentiated regional policies, Angola's independence had been severely limited, Namibia remained a domestic colony, and even Zimbabwe and Zambia became subject to the intruding tentacles of South African influence. In extending its strategic reach, South Africa demonstrated that it was stronger and could act more decisively in its own region in furtherance of its own interests than could any of the interested global powers. It had flexed its military muscle in ways that the Soviet Union could not. It showed how readily the preferences of the West could be denied and the stipulations of the United States, in particular, ignored.

By mid-decade South Africa was stronger within its region than ever before. It could dictate, or at least strongly affect, the political, economic, and logistical decisions of its neighbors. It listened little to the exhortations of the United States and hardly feared expressions of Soviet displeasure. Acting with impunity within the region, and even extending its economic ambit beyond, to the offshore islands and into eastern and West Africa, South Africa by mid-decade had achieved a number of striking strategic breakthroughs and had audaciously seized the regional initiative in a manner that would have been unthinkable a few years before. In the defense of the South African realm, its strategists and tacticians had mounted a broad-ranging, highly manipulative attack against the weak and weakened states around South Africa's periphery, and, having achieved a series of unexpectedly clear victories, proceeded during the remainder of the early 1980s to assail the enemy—the African National Congress (ANC) and South West Africa People's Organization (SWAPO) guerrillas and their Soviet, East European, and Cuban backers—in their forward and then their rear redoubts. Taking this offensive to its logical extreme, South Africa sought with increasing success to deny the guerrilla movements what had hitherto been zones of sanctuary in the larger nations of the region. Further, as an added component of its regional offensive, South Africa systematically used economic and military coercion and political and economic cajolery to humble as well as to destroy the abilities of these states to act autonomously in policy areas of concern to South Africa. Thus, even the socialist and Marxist-Leninist states have come under South Africa's sway with a decisiveness that is certain to grow throughout the second half of the 1980s.

The visitation of natural calamity helped. The usual rains diminished in quantity during the early and mid-1980s. Namibia was much more desiccated than usual, Botswana and Zambia were hard hit, and hunger caused by drought became intense in Zimbabwe and Mozambique. In the last, the makings of a disaster were apparent as early as the end of 1983. A month later a once-in-a-lifetime cyclone felled crops and paralyzed the countryside. Thereafter, the rains stopped completely. By the end of 1984 a million or more Mozambiquans were starving. Zimbabwe, the region's granary, was for the second year itself short of maize, and only nearby Malawi had a small surplus. But South African–inspired unrest in the Mozambiquan countryside made the distribution of grain problematic, even if enough could be purchased by a poor country made weaker by drought and relentless South African pressure.

Mozambique, more signally and severely than others in the region, but possibly as their precursor, had been forced figuratively and diplomatically to supplicate itself before the might of South Africa. Independent since 1975 and a Soviet-supported, officially Marxist-Leninist outpost for nearly a decade, Mozambique in 1984 signed a peace pact with South Africa; ousted the ANC from its prominent position within the country; and eagerly sought a new, cozy, economically and politically advantageous relationship with the big neighbor that it had previously always reviled with vigor. This precedent-shattering public acknowledgment of the success of South Africa's regional offensive was a product of severe economic reverses, which stemmed from local mismanagement and falling export prices for Mozambique's few agricultural commodities; from the drought; and from an unremitting and ultimately over-weening effort by South Africa to destabilize the country and, indeed, the region as a whole.

One point of view, shared by foreign critics as well as politically influential white South Africans, is that South Africa's most durable long-term security depends upon bolstering the stability of southern Africa as a whole, and its fragile nations individually and collectively. Their prosperity would, particularly in still tentatively multiracial Zimbabwe, de-radicalize the cutting edge of their black leadership cadres and inevitably focus the attention of those cadres and their countries on economic growth and internal rather than external political struggles and adventures. If white South Africa were determined to maximize its own chances of avoiding an abrupt shift in power at home, helping its neighbors to develop, and in the process employing South Africa's potentially vast regional economic leverage (as well as assistance), it could most effectively deny outsiders such as the Soviet Union and radically minded internal antagonists opportunities to gain a significant position in or hold on the region.

Those who argue that prosperity and stability in the neighborhood would prove positive attributes think defensively. They may also see virtue internationally in the pursuit of such objectives, and assume that any other course of action will draw Western ire and retribution. Whatever the theoretical logic and ethical validity of a policy designed to contribute to the stability of the black states surrounding South Africa, those who have governed South Africa since the late 1970s, and whose power has grown during the 1980s, believed a different, more aggressive policy of subversion would accomplish the objectives of the ruling party of South Africa with greater certainty. Despite the possibility that their initiatives would attract the opprobrium of the West and the militancy of the Soviet Union and its proxies, and might be expensive and unnecessarily dangerous, the architects of South Africa's new regional thrust of the 1980s decided that they could defend their country's self-interest best by destabilizing the countries of southern Africa. By weakening the new ruling groups, by making their countries and their economies subject to steady undermining by South African–funded and armed initiatives and/or economic reprisals, these architects saw South Africa gain strength while every other country in the region became weaker.

The experimentation with and then the wholesale employment of destabilization as a strategic instrument paralleled the growth within South Africa of the influence on national policy of the military, and in particular of the reorganization of the country's decision-making machinery to reflect and advance that influence. Since the early 1980s, as chapter 2, "Decision Making and the Military," shows, military thinking and military methods have become more central than ever before to the thinking of the upper echelons of South Africa's bureaucracy. Given the military's role in the organization and working of the State Security Council; the ties of the military establishment to President Pieter W. Botha, for thirteen years minister of defense before he became prime minister in 1978; the perception of increased danger to the regime in the aftermath of the Soweto riots of 1976–1977; the achievement of independence for Angola and Mozambique in 1975; and the coming to power in Zimbabwe in 1980 of the revolutionary party that South Africa had strongly—and, in theory, cleverly and successfully—opposed, it is at least explicable that a defense force that had been humbled by a combination of international and political timidity in Angola in 1975–1976 should have welcomed the opportunity to extend its scope and determine external policy in the 1980s.

The South African military and its political masters had essayed destabilization in Angola in 1978 and 1979. Learning from Israel the value of preemptive strikes and presumably testing both Western and Soviet response capabilities, South Africa raided SWAPO camps well behind the Angolan frontier. It began to give massive support to Jonas Savimbi's Union for the Total Independence of Angola (UNITA), which had lost the Angolan civil war of 1975–1976 to the Soviet- and Cuban-backed Movement for the Popular Liberation of Angola (MPLA). After 1980 it also agreed to back an insurgency movement that had originally been funded by the white Rhodesian government in its battle during the 1970s against black guerrillas. That movement, trained from about 1980 in the northern Transvaal, became the Mozambique National Resistance Movement (MNR) and was unleashed against President Samora Machel's Marxist government during the 1980s.

But it was only after President Reagan took office in 1981 that destabilization became South Africa's first line of defense. Constructive engagement, as the approach to South Africa of the Reagan administration was termed, and, as discussed in chapter 8 of this book, provided no hindrance to a broad and assertive expansion of the destabilization initiative. Encouraged on the one hand by the Reagan administration's desire to weaken the Marxist ties of both Angola and Mozambique, and emboldened on the other by the understandable but preoccupying U.S. focus on persuading South Africa to free Namibia, destabilization became a policy that gained adherents among the South African military and political establishments with each perceptible weakening of the neighboring states, and with each incremental advance against both the ANC and SWAPO. As the risks associated with destabilization receded, thanks to the staying of a U.S. hand and the inability or unwillingness of the Soviet forces to be inhibitory, so South Africa went beyond experimentation with such tactics to a broad-gauged assault on those states and regimes that resisted South African influence to any significant degree. (The role of the Soviet Union during this period is discussed in two complementary chapters, 3 and 4.)

South Africa's tactics varied. Using helicopters, it raided Maputo and Maseru in search of ANC militants, but also to cow both host countries. It attacked SWAPO and Angolan encampments in Angola in support of its defense of Namibia and also as part of its offensive against a Marxist host. In pursuit of the same goal, it provided air cover, lavish logistical backing, and—according to well-authenticated reports—direct military assistance for UNITA in its continuing attempt to erode the MPLA's grip on the Angolan countryside. It promoted the MNR and supplied it with weapons and funds sufficient, by later 1983, decisively to loosen the Machel government's grip on the Mozambiquan countryside.

The government of Zimbabwe has accused South Africa of backing the Ndebele rebels who pillaged, murdered, and created untold disorder in the southwestern section of the country from 1981 to 1984. It was also assumed that South Africa was behind other attempts to subvert the new nation, including the destruction of air force fighting planes, sabotage at other military installations, and the assassination of ANC leaders.

Little Lesotho is sure that the Lesotho Liberation Army (LLA)—ironically, led since the 1970s by Ntsu Mokhehle, an old-line nationalist of Marxist persuasion—has continued to exist only because of South African patronage. Since Lesotho is completely surrounded by South Africa (including a South African satrapy), it is hard to fault Lesotho's official suspicion that the LLA, which periodically attacks Lesotho, is on a South African leash, and does the bigger country's bidding as well as its own. But in order to emphasize the clear domination of South Africa and its insistence during the early 1980s that Lesotho should refrain from harboring ANC cadres, refuse to let ANC guerrillas transit its mountainous domain en route to South Africa's cities, and end its rhetorical antagonism to apartheid, South Africa also exerted rather pointed economic pressure on Lesotho through its control of border crossings and employment opportunities for Lesotho's labor, the impoverished small nation's major source of foreign exchange.

Swaziland is as small as Lesotho, but much wealthier. Before and into the 1980s, during the long reign of King Sobhuza II, Swaziland allied itself with South Africa but gave quiet refuge to the ANC and interfered little with the passage of guerrillas from Mozambique into the Transvaal. (Mbabane, Swaziland's tiny capital, is 300 miles from Johannesburg, South Africa's most populous and industrialized metropolitan area.) After

Sobhuza died at eighty-three in 1982, however, South Africa used its financial muscle to gain an even greater influence amid the several parties that merged to become his effective political and economic successor. With South Africa's support, a group of chiefs and ambitious commoners within the Liqoqo gained day-to-day control of the monarchy. At their behest, Swaziland in 1983 secretly signed a nonaggression pact with South Africa and began moving vigorously against the ANC. That approach was broadened during 1984, and the secret agreement made known. Despite opposition within the kingdom to the cabal that ruled the country to mid-decade, and despite outspoken opposition to the state's pro–South African policy, South Africa had succeeded by late 1984 in cementing a friendship with a small neighbor by traditional economic rather than the military means that have been used elsewhere. It had thus managed to block one of the ANC's main routes toward the heart of South Africa, even if—despite Swazi cooperation—it could not claim completely to have staunched the flow of ANC men and materiel in that direction.

By the end of 1984, Lesotho constituted an equal triumph for South Africa, since direct retaliatory strikes (the raid on Maseru); conscious destabilization (backing the LLA, and possibly directing the LLA as well); and the employment of economic leverage (closing the border) had compelled Lesotho to send the ANC packing and attempt to prevent the ANC's free use of Lesotho as a transit zone.

Botswana, equally weak and vulnerable to South Africa, had—before the 1980s—denied the ANC free rein and easy movement across its terrain. The threat of South African retaliation was always there, and Botswana behaved accordingly. In 1984, however, South Africa attempted to bring Botswana even further into line. It attempted to persuade—if that is the correct verb—Botswana to sign a nonaggression pact similar to those with Swaziland and Mozambique. But South Africa by early 1985 had not retaliated against a reluctant government of Botswana by fostering an internal dissident movement or seeking, so far as is known, to destabilize its usually calm and correct neighbor.

Because of their economic relations and degree of dependence upon South Africa and, in Malawi's case, for ideological reasons as well, neither Malawi nor Zambia has been the focus of much South African military attention during the 1980s. Moreover, both countries are too distant geographically from South Africa for any support they might give the ANC to matter terribly to South Africa. Thus, in this decade, Zambia's giving shelter to the political arms, and sometimes the militant arms, of the ANC and SWAPO has not drawn the kind of South African assault that such behavior occasioned during the 1970s. From South Africa's point of view, however, the hard lessons of the 1970s were learned well by Zambia.

More recently, South Africa has been attempting to give Angola the same instruction, with considerable success. Because of the way in which South Africa was permitted to attack Angolan territory with impunity in the 1980s, and given the lack of effective local and world opposition to South Africa's open occupation of a large swath of southern Angola from 1981 through the end of 1984, SWAPO's ability to attack Namibia easily has been curtailed, and Angola has been diminished in spirit as well as in authority. When this expression of military might is added to the massive support for UNITA—which by 1984 was acknowledged to have as many men under arms, and as well trained and equipped, as the MPLA's regular army—South Africa's suzerainty in the area and its influence over Angola by the end of 1984 was impressive if still less than paramount. What was unexpected, and which came about for reasons examined at length in chapters 3 and 4, was the total collapse in 1984 of the retaliatory threat there of the Soviet Union and its proxies.

As the 1980s continue, Angola will sooner or later disentangle itself from the Leninist embrace that has deterred its economic development. It will dismiss the Cubans and then follow, if less slavishly, Mozambique and other nations of the region into greater dependence on South Africa. In order for this process to take its natural course, however, the United States (acting as facilitator and broker as described in chapter 8) will need to find a way of reassuring the MPLA government of Angola that a Cuban exodus and a cutting of ties to the Soviets will not automatically result in the MPLA's loss of control to UNITA, either militarily or through the expedient of a coalition government. Committing such political suicide is obviously too much to ask of any elite, even if its country's economic and political situation has become more and more desperate.

Angola in 1984 began to display a willingness to dismiss the Cubans if that action could trigger the long-awaited creation of an independent Namibia. (The Namibian political situation and the recent U.S. involvement with its outcome is analyzed in chapter 7.) The United States has been telling the Angolans and the world that only the continued presence of 30,600 Cubans prevents South Africa from agreeing to a transfer of power in Namibia, which would probably bring a SWAPO-dominated black group to power. The United States has also assured the Angolans that the independence of Namibia would detach South Africa from UNITA, and thus presumably diminish the effectiveness of UNITA as a fighting force capable of overcoming the MPLA. From the point of view of the Reagan administration, only Angolan trust (and the promise of U.S. recognition and economic assistance in the process) would permit a deescalation of the war that engulfs that nation and an end to the thralldom of Namibia. Possibly the Angolans will have no alternative in the mid-1980s but to put their faith in the U.S.-brokered initiative. Possibly there is no other way to end the civil war and end the economic and political weakness of the country. Possibly, too, the MPLA is confident of its political message and its own military capabilities. But the answer to Namibia's freedom and the reclaiming of Angolan independence is equally in South Africa's power to give. Strengthened by constructive engagement in ways that are discussed in chapter 8, emboldened by the success of destabilization, and immeasurably more powerful in its region in early 1985 than it was in 1980 or before, South Africa may have little incentive from a regional-security point of view to accede to the United States' and United Nations' wishes concerning Namibia or Angola. The value of Namibia to South Africa has become greater rather than smaller since the early 1980s, as explained in chapter 7. To ask South Africa to abandon UNITA and Namibia at a time when South Africa is more secure and more brash than ever before may be asking more than the West can accomplish. The neighborhood is too weak, and South Africa too strong.

In 1984, when Pretoria claimed Mozambique as a client, destabilization—hitherto strenuously denied as a conscious South African policy, particularly with regard to the MNR and the LLA—came out of the closet. The agreement between the two nations in early 1984 should have ended South African support for the MNR, but clandestine logistical and financial assistance kept the politically inert but militarily effective movement vigorously active throughout the remainder of the year. Their 15,000 men about equaled the number of soldiers in the Mozambiquan army. An authoritative account described how thoroughly the MNR had impaired the functioning of the desperate country: "No road or rail line beyond the limits of Mozambique's cities and towns is safe from mining and ambushes; no Government installation in the countryside—school, clinic, shop, or administrative building—is immune to hit-and-run raids."[1]

At the end of 1984 Mozambique was virtually without means. Lacking foreign exchange and heavily in debt, it even rationed food in its cities. Unable to keep its people alive without international assistance, devoid of funds with which to obtain fuel or basic consumer imports, and convulsed by the depredations of the MNR, Mozambique had benefited little from its détente with South Africa. Its leaders openly suspected that South Africa, or at least a section of its army, had continued—all public pronouncements to the contrary—to favor further destabilization. South Africa may have wished to extract the last ounce of compliance from a Mozambique supine and still clinging to Marxism. Earlier South Africa had wanted to overthrow Machel and his government, but by late 1984 a skeptic could conclude plausibly that South Africa was using Mozambique's plight to demonstrate to the region and to the Soviets how thoroughly South Africa could dominate southern Africa. Moreover, South Africa may have desired more than the acquisition of a common client—may, in fact, have sought ways of exerting total control over Mozambique's destiny.

Destabilization originally was an additional weapon in South Africa's perimeter defense. Then it became part of an offensive endeavor that could enhance South Africa's regional position. From 1984, with the ANC and SWAPO forced to withdraw from their bases near South Africa to more distant bastions in the continent's interior, South Africa could concentrate upon furthering its own vision of a region dominated by a white-run South Africa. Weakening Mozambique irredeemably was essential, as was the continued humbling of the small states, of Zimbabwe, and—as much as possible—of Angola and a future Namibia.

Yet in its moment of unquestioned regional hegemony, the palpable softness of the core was again revealed. As South Africa shifted in late 1984 from a parliamentary to a presidential system; as, albeit after two low and disputed polls, it incorporated Coloured and Asian representatives into a tricameral legislature and thus broadened the ethnic complexion of its governing elite; so white South Africa reemphasized the total exclusion of the nation's African majority from all participation in the affairs of the central government of the country. Minority rule was reiterated, with doors slammed shut on African aspirations for the future. It was in that volatile political context, with adolescents still agitating against an inferior and unequal educational system—and after a winter punctuated by severely increased prices for consumer staples such as maize meal, bread, and cooking oil—that black township authorities began attempting to collect house rents that had been raised by about 25 percent. First, south of Johannesburg in the Vereeniging area, and then east of Johannesburg in and around Tembisa, and finally in Soweto to the west of the city, Africans rioted during September, October, and November. More than 500 Africans lost their lives, thousands were wounded, and hundreds were arrested by the police. Finally, in desperation, the government moved the army into a number of townships and also arrested union leaders. Still the violence continued, most of it directed by Africans at fellow Africans collaborating with the apartheid system.

Strong regionally, South Africa was still hollow within. Even its army could not easily contain the riots. Moreover, the violence demonstrated more clearly than could even the verbal protests of Bishop Desmond

Tutu, the winner of the 1984 Nobel Peace Prize, and others, that Africans expected to derive little benefit from the reform initiative that had been trumpeted by President Botha and other leading whites, had led to the establishment of Coloured and Asian chambers in the parliament, and had been heralded by the U.S. State Department. Indeed, the message of the riots was that Africans derided the reform initiative, viewed it as merely cosmetic, and understood more perfectly than outsiders that whites were still unwilling to share power with blacks or to make any meaningful political concessions to the country's majority.

The continuing struggle between white and black in South Africa is not the primary subject of this book. Instead, as an outgrowth of a conference on the regional security of southern Africa, which was held in South Africa in 1984 under the auspices of the World Peace Foundation of Boston and the South African Institute of International Affairs of Johannesburg, it is largely about South Africa's emerging dominance of its region and the consequences of that dominance for the future of southern Africa. The two chapters on the role of the Soviet Union take the measure of South Africa's military rival, and, in somewhat different ways, evaluate how important Soviet influence in this sphere has been and can be. Both chapters show that the Soviet "total onslaught," so craftily employed by white South Africa to bolster its defenses, never existed and does not represent a credible future threat. The two chapters on the economic foundations of regional policy demonstrate the extent to which South Africa has come to control the economic destinies of the region, and how that very dominance provides opportunities as well as innumerable and serious constraints for the countries of the region and their two new transnational economic organizations. A fifth chapter examines the obstacles to an easy or rapid resolution of the Namibian problem. That chapter is linked with the critique in the final chapter of constructive engagement as an instrument of progressive change in southern Africa. That chapter ends where this introduction begins: U.S. policy and Soviet weakness have joined natural disasters to emphasize the attributes of South African hegemony within its geographical region.

How South Africa employs its new regional position, whether and how the United States attempts to encourage South Africa to use its undoubted dominance to strengthen and not undermine the weaker countries of the region, and whether and how the United States can finally commit South Africa to freeing Namibia, are questions that a later book will doubtless explore. In the mid-1980s, positive answers to the Namibian and other questions might well come from the weakness within South Africa. New riots have exposed that vulnerability, and the national economic crisis of 1983–1985 has amplified its consequences for the state and for its white minority.

It is not that South Africa had become ungovernable by 1985. Rather, in order to build upon its regional strength, South Africa would in the later 1980s have to eliminate the sources of danger within the fortress. Only by evolving rapidly and modernizing its political structure could South Africa remain a truly regional power and continue to enjoy the full range of economic advantage that may ultimately provide stability and developmental opportunities for all parts of southern Africa. Security, in the final analysis, cannot be assured by instability and starvation. Nor is the elimination of Soviet opportunism, destabilization, chaos, clientage, and the holding hostage of fragile nations likely in conditions of insecurity.

Note

1. Henry Kamm, "Deadly Famine in Mozambique Called Inevitable," *The New York Times,* 18 November 1984.

2

Decision Making and the Military in South Africa

Robert I. Rotberg

The process by which any institution arrives at decisions determines the array and quality of its answers and, more important, the range, nature, scope, focus, and internal honesty of those answers. It is a truism that, without good questions, an institution produces good answers only by chance. With sufficient answers and wrong or irrelevant questions, the capacity of the institution to make decisions in any coherent fashion must obviously be limited. When the institution in question is a modern state—particularly a regionally powerful, ethnically divided, plural society where a comparatively small minority rules and intends indefinitely to rule a far larger and antagonized majority—the manner in which decisions are or are not reached becomes crucial if outsiders are fully to understand the way in which that state has organized its capacity to act, including the immediately salient components of information gathering, option building, hypothesis testing, and implementation.

With an appreciation of the process by which decisions are being reached, estimates are possible of internal flexibility and intransigence, susceptibility to influence, crucial organizing principles, critical individuals, and how each component or factor interacts with the others to help manage the complicated organization and governance of a nation. When the state in question is South Africa, and when the extent to which South Africa is now intent on the massive modernization of its methods of governmental operation is known, then the issue of decision making becomes ever more central to those who want to encourage one or more directions to that modernization.

Now that South Africa has adopted a new constitution giving a state president potentially authoritarian powers, the State Security Council, which this chapter describes, has become even more important than the cabinet that guides the new tricameral parliament. In the new state, the power to make decisions is constitutionally focused in the office of the president. The council is well placed to advise and guide a strong-minded president. It implements his decisions. In both capacities, it continues to function as a military-dominated, technocratically based guiding arm of the nation. Under the new system, which is praetorian by intent, the council is structurally placed to extend its already great reach and increase its influence on all kinds of decisions, as well as the very process by which the most critical decisions will be made.

Before Botha

Two elements epitomize the striking differences between South African decision making before and after 1980: (1) There now is a formal mechanism intended to apply to the entire system of national government; (2) the military fuels and lubricates this mechanism, and is largely responsible for its momentum and direction.

Before 1980, especially during the twelve-year prime ministership of B. Johannes Vorster, South Africa came to conclusions in an unmethodical manner. Vorster, although rigid in personality and dominant as an unquestioned, authoritarian leader, believed in a decentralized style of management. Cabinet ministers conformed to the overall policies set by Vorster and a small oligarchy, and in some areas those of the National party and the Broederbond. Within that conformity to an overall plan, however, ministers were encouraged to run their departments with little interference from the prime minister. Such autonomy stimulated political competition among departments. Often ministries were kept ignorant of what others were doing or planning. Collective responsibility was difficult to impose. In practice, there were no instruments, other than personal appeals to the prime minister, to limit this competition or to coordinate the different, sometimes cross-cutting, affairs of state. Perhaps Vorster, like Prime Minister Hendrik Verwoerd before him, welcomed the rivalries. More plausibly, the absence of coordination and the accompanying slovenly administrative style were carried over from earlier times, when the meshing of the initiatives of one or more departments may have been less critical to the functioning of the state.

For Vorster and his predecessors, informal methods generally produced sufficient results. Furthermore, a decentralized state machinery accentuated the personal power of the prime minister, backed as he would always have been by personal alliances, party prerogatives, and largely unchallenged control over the distribution of patronage and preferment. In a regimented society with common political goals represented by an unadventuresome party caucus and held together by the imposition of discipline from a secret society and an allied church, the government functioned naturally as an assemblage of personalized and well-demarcated fiefdoms.

In Vorster's day, some of the departments, not the cabinet as a collectivity, were given (or demanded) command of the grand overarching policy initiatives of the state. Bantu Administration (since then Plural Development and Cooperation and Development) was charged with devising and seeing through the transformation of Bantustans into quasi-autonomous homelands. The Information Department had its various forms of outreach and propaganda peddling, some clandestine and some not, and was almost immune from interference by Foreign Affairs. Finance operated largely on its own, as did Sport and other ministries, except when fundamental decisions had to be reached. At that point, either Vorster alone or Vorster and several cabinet and/or nongovermental colleagues arrived at decisions on the basis of information provided (depending on the issue) by a single or by competing departments, or by the state's security apparatus.

General Hendrik van den Bergh was Vorster's closest confidant and a devoted adviser from the days of their internment at Koffiefontein in World War II. Van den Bergh, a security policeman, fashioned the secret Republican Intelligence group out of the security police, which he headed, when Vorster was minister of justice under Verwoerd in the early 1960s. Republican Intelligence was created at a time when the African National Congress, the Pan-Africanist Congress, and the Communist party had all been driven underground and were challenging the state with violence. There was an external threat, too, for the outside world was becoming increasingly hostile. Van den Bergh organized the Republican Intelligence to gather information at home and abroad, to engage where necessary in espionage, and to strengthen the hand of those—like Vorster—who were determined to outwit local and foreign rivals.

In 1969 the still-clandestine Republican Intelligence formed the nucleus of the new Bureau of State Security (BOSS), a department of state. BOSS attempted with some success to usurp the prime functions of the security police and military intelligence. As security adviser to Vorster, van den Bergh had great organizational advantages to add to those that derived from his long friendship with the prime minister. He made much of these advantages, but they won no friends among the police or the military, especially among the latter (whose minister throughout this period was Pieter W. Botha).

BOSS doubled in size during its first ten years, and van den Bergh exercised more informal power than most South Africans realized. Along with Connie Mulder, the minister of information, of interior, and of Bantu Administration (Plural Development), he helped plan and implement the policy of reaching out to Africans, of trading with them, of bribing or compromising foreigners of all kinds, of working effectively with Israel, and of (paradoxically) reforming South Africa's overseas image while simultaneously eradicating dissent at home. Van den Bergh opposed the Defence Force on the efficacy of what would now be called destabilization, and particularly over the invasion of Angola.

Van den Bergh's decisive influence is now widely known. What is less fully appreciated, however, is the extent to which BOSS, under van den Bergh's direction, provided much of what little machinery of coordination existed during the Vorster era. Yet, as rudimentary as was that machinery, it was in many respects much more significant, even powerful, than the formal apparatus that now exists. Van den Bergh was the crisis manager. With Vorster's blessing, and presumably at his behest, he dealt with emergencies and coordinated responses. As those crises became more and more charged and frequent, he and BOSS were more and more at the center of decision making in the Vorster era. How smoothly crises were managed is another question. Van den Bergh was an autocrat, and building a consensus was neither his talent nor his immediate responsibility. But he did compel the diverse tentacles of the state to come to grips with problems that overwhelmed individual ministries and, at times, threatened to overwhelm the state.

Informal techniques, unclear accounting, and administrative obscurantism have their uses, especially when a modern nation attempts to gain what the leaders regard as just ends by questionable means, or by means that the public would question if it only knew. In the case of South Africa under Vorster, the lack of a centralized, formal mechanism of decision making facilitated the hodgepodge of covert activities that eventually brought Vorster (as well as van den Bergh and Mulder) into disrepute and ended their control of the government. The great affairs of state, it transpired, had been decided by cronies huddling together and writing directives on the backs of envelopes. The so-called Infogate, or Muldergate, scandal brought new people to power. It also mandated the search for a new system of decision making that, ideally, would provide better and more comprehensive information on the basis of which decisions could rationally be made; would provide a means to organize that information; and would offer a framework capable of deciding which among the many questions required information, and of what kind. Coordination of the process was necessary. If these various elements were effectively meshed, then coordinating the implementation of the ultimate decisions would, it was thought, be made both more systematic and more logical than before.

Total Onslaught and Total Strategy

An alternative apparatus already existed. Following a set of recommendations made by Justice Potgeiter in 1972, the Security, Intelligence and

State Security Council Act, #64, was passed in the same year. It provided for a State Security Council (SSC), but until 1979 the SSC was only one of twenty cabinet committees. Vorster paid little attention to any of them, their meetings were irregular and infrequent, their agendas were uncirculated, and no minutes were kept (nor were minutes kept of cabinet meetings).

When Botha became prime minister, he needed—not least for political reasons—to assert control over BOSS, over what remained of Mulder's empire, and over what he correctly regarded as an upper- and middle-level bureaucracy that might well be loyal to Vorster. The military had scores to settle, too. In addition, since the Angolan invasion in 1975, if not earlier, its analysis of how best to deal with South Africa's enemies had been at variance with cabinet policy. Its leaders, and Botha, had wanted to take the war to the enemy. Influenced by Israeli strategic doctrine, and smarting from their humiliation in Angola, they were anxious to take charge. Moreover, Botha, along with his military advisers, had for thirteen years been running a ministry in an orderly manner. Given a sense of managerial pride, Botha's own instincts as a party technocrat, a degree of militaristic scorn for the slough into which the country had stumbled—arguably because of poor administrative methods, the scandal, and the prevalent military assessment (which Botha shared) of what the future held for an unreformed South Africa—it is no wonder that a new prime minister decided to centralize, streamline, and reorient the way in which the decision-making machinery of the state would be organized.

Botha was the first prime minister to recognize publicly that revolution was a real possibility. In order to implement an effective counter-revolutionary strategy, the state needed to function effectively, as a disciplined unit (to use a conscious military metaphor). "Total onslaught," quickly became the code name used by Botha, General Magnus Malan, and others from the military establishment to describe the Soviet war-mongers, antiapartheid activists, and anyone else willing to support the African National Congress or other guerrilla movements in antagonizing South Africa. Malan first articulated the tenets of total strategy in 1977: "In a mature state the fundamental concepts of conflict entail far more than war. It means the formulation of national objectives in which all the community's resources are mustered and managed on a coordinated level to ensure survival. Every activity of the state must be seen and understood as a function of total war." Malan defined total war as something in which South Africa was already engaged: "As long as we are not fighting back we are losing."[1] The onslaught, said Malan, was militaristic, political, diplomatic, religious, psychological, cultural, and social. It was an "ideologically motivated struggle and the aim is the implacable and unconditional imposition of the aggressor's will on the target state."[2] Only a total response could meet the total onslaught, and a smoothly functioning form of coordination was a necessary component of the total response. Moreover, when a state is assaulted totally, everything with which the government might conceivably concern itself becomes fit subject for concerted state study, analysis, and policy guidance.

There is a further consideration that may directly or indirectly have brought not only Botha but a range of other Afrikaner power-wielders to a recognition that some new method was necessary if apartheid were to make the survival of the *volk* likely, even realistic, in a changing and troubled world. Apartheid had begun to lose its internal legitimacy—what some have called its hegemonic character and appeal.[3] If so, or if the rethinking of the validity as well as the efficacy of radical discrimination and separate development by new Afrikaners (*verlighte* ones, if that concept is helpful) had focused the prime minister's ideas, that line of analysis had also entered the military mind. A new ethic was defined as survival through modernization, but not by challenging the very foundations of Afrikaner power. What Botha and officers alike chose to counter the apartheid state's loss of hegemony was an instrumental formalism—a rationalized pragmatism of which the chosen instrument, naturally, was a new administrative structure and an important shift in the locus of decision-making power from old-line bureaucrats to a cadre of militarily trained technocrats.[4]

Botha announced his sweeping administrative reforms in 1979. Although the full intent of these changes was not realized until 1983, the shift from twenty to four cabinet committees, the primacy given formally and informally to the refurbished SSC, the concomitant expansion of the Department of the Prime Minister (later the Office of the President) and the creation of a cabinet secretariat, the distribution of agendas and the keeping of minutes, the punctiliousness with which paper flow was regulated, and the role that the military played in the entire process transformed South Africa's method of accomplishing and its ability to accomplish its business.

The new South African executive presidency is at least nominally responsible to the country's new parliament. However, the instruments of the new formalism bypassed the old cabinet and parliament to a degree that was new for South Africa. If this process serves South Africa well in the future, it will do so by elevating the goals of bureaucratic achievement and policy coordination above those of meaningful political participation and the open development of a national consensus.

The State Security Council

At the heart of the new management system, and central to all of Botha's plans for himself, his government, and his country, is the State Security

Council. It meets every Monday, in session and out, functioning during the sitting of parliament as a kind of executive committee and, crucially, during the many months when parliamentarians are dispersed, as the only regularly functioning locus of authority. The president chairs the meetings. He is joined by the leading cabinet ministers. Further regular members are the directors-general of foreign affairs and justice, the head of the police, the commander of the Defence Force, and the director of the National Intelligence Service (NIS). Other individuals are invited from time to time to address or meet with the SSC. The SSC takes its decisions by consensus, but the formation of a consensus usually follows the lead of the president.

What is immediately apparent is the number of ministers, mostly junior in status, who are not members of the SSC. Furthermore, the notion of cabinet responsibility and their own positions as ministers are devalued within the government by the presence of the innermost state decision-making councils of nonelected officials, three of whom are responsible for implementing the so-called total strategy. The composition of the SSC, as much as the president's command of it, narrows the government's legislative focus and also preordains the kinds of subjects that are addressed as well as the approach to each. Additionally, given its size, status, and direction, the SSC's concerns and its conclusions inevitably influence, inhibit, and overshadow the cabinet committees as well as the entire functioning of the Botha government.

If its subject matter and membership did not give the SSC a preeminent status in the government, it would be able to achieve significant leverage by virtue of its size, organization, and bureaucratic resources. The secretary of the SSC commands the working committee (which corresponds to the working groups of the other committees) of the SSC, which itself is composed primarily of officials from the military and police departments, justice, and foreign affairs. But the secretary also has a staff, which serves him and which is nine times the size of the staffs serving the other cabinet committees.

The secretary monitors everything that goes on at the cabinet and subcabinet level. He sits as a member of the working groups of the three other cabinet committees and shares the responsibility for reviewing and channeling all policy papers destined for subcabinet or cabinet consideration.

Below the secretariat, and also subordinate to the working groups and the working committee, are interdepartmental committees. They emanate from and report to the SSC organizationally, and are the originators of nearly all policy recommendations. The membership of the interdepartmental committees consists principally of heads of departments and of their senior deputies, legal advisers, and so on. A representative of the Defence Ministry sits on each committee. Foreign Affairs is represented only on four of the interdepartmental committees, other ministries by no more than and usually less than that number.

The military mind has imposed itself on the workings of the South African government, but the nature and quality of that mind should first be seen as technocratic and functional and not, by the medium of the SSC, as a collectivity with (as yet) Latin American–type designs on the transformation or the capture of the state. Those kinds of prescriptive possibilities have doubtless occurred to many officers now serving at the heart of the bureaucratic endeavor, particularly if they have viewed inefficiency and—perish the thought—chicanery in the ranks of civilian government. The managerial revolution, however, is still a servant of a more cautious, politically led reorientation of South Africa's primary direction.

The SSC effectively makes decisions and influences many that are not directly its own. As its name implies, all security (military and police) questions are brought to it. Since, according to the South African doctrine of total onslaught and total strategy, this rubric is subject necessarily to a very broad interpretation, almost every aspect of modern government in South Africa can be construed to have security implications. The set of the military mind has permeated Botha's government and will continue to do so. It proliferates via the interdepartmental committees, the secretariat, and the working groups. Moreover—and much more basic to an understanding of who runs South Africa today, and how it may continue to run—the SSC has become the court of virtually final resort for a broad range of national issues.

The future of Namibia is hardly a matter of parochial concern. It is a bundle of domestic and external political issues, questions involving intricate negotiations with the West and with Angola, tactics for counterrevolutionary action within the territory and across its borders, economic and financial concerns, social matters, and so on. How South Africa resolves the problem of Namibia has a direct impact, one would think, on the entire future security, economic well-being, and political survival of white South Africa itself. Yet, if the fate of Namibia were ever an issue discussed by the representatives of even the white electorate of South Africa, that day is past. Strategy and tactics with respect to Namibia are decided upon in the SSC whenever those decisions have not hitherto been preempted by a military action of some kind. Did the military decide to undo Dirk Mudge, leader of the Democratic Turnhalle Alliance, before or after a decision was taken in the SSC? Was the decision to back Peter Kalangula of the National Democratic Congress a decision made in Namibia by the army, or by the SSC? The SSC probably has authorized the overall direction of preemptive strikes into Angola, leaving a chain of military command to work out the precise details. It regulates the flow of supplies to UNITA. It sanctioned the cease-fire talks with Angola. It decides how and when to respond to Western initiatives. Important, too, each decision of this kind began, whether implicitly or actually, as an option presented to the SSC. The positions on which the options were based started as military or, sometimes, foreign affairs initiatives.

The range of possibilities presented to the SSC need not emerge from the deliberations of the working committee in especially broad forms. The influence of doves, such as the foreign minister and his director-general, are limited by the preponderance of hawks at all levels of this new decision-making apparatus. From a structural viewpoint, personalities aside, it is easy to understand why the foreign ministry should feel so powerless beside the juggernaut of the technocratic, military machine.

Whether to raid Maseru, support the Mozambique National Resistance Movement (MNR), give aid to Zimbabwean dissidents, and try to purchase long-range reconnaissance aircraft are obviously decisions within the ultimate purview of the SSC. In the case of the Maseru raid, for example, the Defence Force seems to have had prior approval in principle from the SSC. The cabinet, however, was not informed beforehand, and the Defence Force probably chose the precise date and method in accord with general rather than specific instructions.

The SSC involves itself in a much broader range of decisions, too. It is interested in land transfers such as the attempt to cede KaNgwane and part of Ingwavumaland to Swaziland. It has a say about the overall policy regarding trade unions, detentions without trial, the shape of new Defence-Force legislation (including the conscientious objectors), the character of social legislation (particularly that giving further prerogatives to Africans), and the broadening of the educational franchise.

Who Governs?

The formal mechanism of decision making in South Africa gives the SSC a primary role and the three other cabinet committees important but (except for the Finance and Economics Committee) lesser ones. Because the SSC and the other committees are subject to direct and indirect influence by well-entrenched civil servants, and since so many of those civil servants are in fact seconded military officers, it is evident that the real levers of formal power in South Africa are no longer controlled exclusively, as much as they were—or as much as the South African public may think that they are—by elected representatives of the (white) people. Indeed, the National Defence Management System has superseded the cabinet, the party, and the electorate in many areas. A saving grace, if that is the word, is that the president is in ultimate control, assisted by at least one other elected party member, and the chain of military command. Furthermore, as a clear hindrance to complete military dominance of the decision-making machinery, there is the undoubted awareness by nonmilitary bureaucrats of their precarious, weakened position; a suspicion of military designs; and the natural infighting of one institution that has been invaded by another. This internecine warfare may help to limit the influence of the military. The factor of jealousy may operate, too, in a manner that gives ground only grudgingly to the military inside the edifice of South African decision making.

Nevertheless, if the cabinet is weaker and, in most respects, titular in its authority, the National party has lost power dramatically. There still are parliamentary study committees on virtually all subjects; their chairmen (back-bench members of the National party) once could hold ministers to account. Such success is now more difficult to achieve, however, and the whips easily bring defectors to heel. Where the caucus retains much of its power is not on particular decisions but on the very broad reach of national policy. The president cannot risk a revolt among his back-benchers, for example, on a matter such as constitutional reform and the internal organization of the proposed new parliament. He can, however, ignore them over Namibia, over destabilization, over trade unions, and so on. Neither he nor the military bureaucrats can ignore the back-benchers over issues of constituency concern—borehole drilling, perimeter defense, and so on—but that is the essence more of politics than of decision making.

Beyond the caucus of the party are the provincial congresses—the inner core and the strength of the National party. The president has used the provincial machinery skillfully, but he has not sought its advice over security or Namibia. Nor did he ask its permission to hold a referendum on the constitutional proposals. He probably consulted the cabinet, but only after a small-group decision that was ventilated (probably without much staff work) in the SSC. There also are provincial legislatures and officials, but their influence on national or party policy has been diminished under Botha.

Commissions of inquiry, composed of experts, of presumed adjudicators such as judges, or of a cross-section of the power elite, play a role in the South African decision-making process. There have been notable and notorious commissions in South Africa's recent history. The Tomlinson and Theron commissions are in one category; the Cillie, Schlebusch, and Steyn commissions in another (to which Eloff and Rumpff have been added); and the Wiehahn, Riekert, and Grosskopft commissions (joined by De Lange and van de Walt) in still another. Since the formation of commissions is used throughout the world to defer decisions or postpone them permanently, it comes as no surprise that official South Africa has found it expedient from time to time to give intractable problems to supposedly impartial commissions, in the hope that the very calling of a commission will make the problem go away or that the passage of time will make recommendations electorally or internationally palatable. Some commissions have studied a problem and, from the government's view, exceeded their mandate by proposing solutions too radical for the president, the party, the civil service, or all three. Other commissions—mostly those attempting to solve problems in areas where the government knows it must advance, but cannot think how—have, because of a sufficiently broad and influential membership, a decisive and well-connected chairman, or both, altered the perceptions of the government itself.

Some of the academically led commissions can be expected to develop their own sources of information and analysis. Normally, that function is performed by a seconded bureaucracy. Insofar as those seconded staffs will now be drawn, even partially, from the SSC and the military, an additional lever will be added to the influence that the Defence Force wields over the development of South African decision making.

Do the departments themselves still matter? Clearly, no matter how well the SSC and the other committees coordinate, prod, and push, the machinery of implementation remains in the departments. The SSC, through its mostly military representatives, can learn what is happening and why, and can certainly poke and extol the departments through the interdepartmental committees; but the drafting of legislation is still done in departments. Bureaucrats know how to drag their feet and work to rule; they also know and make the regulations. Thus the cooperation of the departments is necessary before decisions can be implemented. So there is a brake on all kinds of decisions outside the sphere of the military or the president's own office. Any decision for which the military has the resources can be implemented rapidly. Thus the departments have lost significant control—but by no means the overwhelming share of their previous power—both to the coordinating machinery and also to the military. They have lost initiatives and a share of the available overall finances, which, in any institutional conflict, go to the favored and the swift, especially if the favored and the swift are guiding the ship of state.

What has been described thus far is the formal process used in South Africa to arrive at decisions. The process is intended to be methodical and systematic, by definition being a formula intolerant of shortcuts. Intentionally painstaking, it can only be worked by an enlarged coordinating bureaucracy. And it takes time, especially if policy directives and actual legislation are to reflect new kinds of degrees of staff attention.

This is a system that could prepare for crises and emergencies but rarely could cope with them in an instantaneous fashion. It may be a system more efficient than the informal one employed in Vorster's day, but it is cumbersome. Therefore, describing and analyzing the formal decision-making capacity and machinery of the South African state can only partially answer the crucial question: Is the new machinery actually employed when those who rule South Africa make the decisions that count?

Vorster and van den Bergh made the important decisions in their time. Vorster also had his golfing friends and corporate cronies. Representives of other kinds of institutions used contacts to reach Vorster himself, either to obtain favorable decisions or to get other forms of help at one or more levels of government. Impressionistic evidence indicates that Vorster gathered most of his ideas, information, and insights from his tight-knit circles of friends. Most of those friends were from the private sector, and Vorster was never loath to bypass official channels. The Muldergate scandal made this point perfectly evident. Vorster's staff work was rudimentary, and his colleagues and his party caucus rarely knew precisely how or why key decisions were made.

Today this process is supposed to be different. But is it? Botha has a new set of friends and is not known for his golf, but he is close to Malan and other military officers. In crises, Malan rushes to Botha's side as van den Bergh went to Vorster. Ad hoc decisions are still made, or at least recorded, on the backs of envelopes. Someone decided to back the attempt to overthrow the government of the Seychelles. It is understood that the SSC did not know about it, although sections of the military and the NIS were aware of the preparations that were revealed in court. The Swaziland swap seems to have been initiated by the upper reaches of the Ministry of Foreign Affairs and never to have been subjected to full SSC or cabinet scrutiny. Responses to U.S. or Angolan negotiating endeavors are probably required too urgently to be left to percolate through each of the levels of the SSC. If swift responses were needed as a result of, say, the ouster of a neighboring head of state, it would be equally difficult to formulate policy through the SSC. Overall, South Africa still lacks what Chester Crocker calls a capacity for sophisticated threat assessment and political analysis.[5]

No modern executive is fully accountable. South Africa's never was and is now supposed to be; but no matter how punctilious the procedures and ironclad the rules, it is hardly plausible that Botha acts only when he has proper briefing books and full analyses. A volatile person, he naturally responds to decisive moments, even if to do so may mean bending his own strictures about the need for "research." Moreover, ad hoc decisions made by Botha; by Malan; by the chief of the Defence Force (for example, the Maseru raid); or even by generals in Namibia/Angola are decisions more important and more injurious than those that usually filter up through the SSC and the other committees.

In noting the distinction between formal and informal modes of decision making and the different kinds of decisions that are made in both spheres, it should also be apparent that the membrane between formal and informal is permeable. The internal impinges upon and influences the formal. The formal validates and covers up for the informal. Presidents are known to come to SSC meetings with their own plans, or plans devised after talking to all manner of outsiders from different parts of the private sector.

Decisions that are unfortunate for South Africa—defined in this context merely as those (like the killing of Steve Biko) that generate unfavorable publicity—need not have been made through formal channels. If a preemptive strike on a neighboring nation infuriates the West, that is one kind of decision where an agreement in principle, made initially at high levels (if not through the stated channels) may become a counterproductive act if the scale, the timing, or the side effects of the strike conform insufficiently to the original policy directive. Moreover, the military leadership may (as in Namibia) have an agenda different from those of most if not all politicians. The entire destabilization policy may fit this rubric. Where South Africa suffers most, however (even under the National Defence Management System), is when middle-level officials react traditionally or exceed instructions. Or it is possible that they obey the letter of outdated or ill-conceived instructions from their superiors. The death of Saul Mkhize, defending his land in the southeastern Transvaal, is an example of a general decision (to continue removals), followed by a high-level decision (one presumes) to move against the particular Driefontein black spot and to ignore African protests, followed by the maladroit implementation of orders by low-ranking bureaucrats. It is unlikely that any management system, no matter how efficient, can rapidly alter the reflexes of officials at modest levels. Moreover, given the structure of South Africa, it is probably too much to expect the National Defence Management System to think through the consequences at the implementational level of all varieties of decisions that flow from a policy framework (in this case apartheid) with so many givens, precedents, and shibboleths. Botha does not intend his new military-manned system to transform South Africa. He merely wants the tactical (not the strategic) posture of his administration to be coherent and coordinated.

Individuals influence decision makers informally. So do institutions. Botha's government is much less influenced by or intertwined with the Broederbond than was Vorster's. The Kerk has declined in its immediate influence on the leaders of the present government, and nationally as well. The Afrikaans-speaking business community has access to Botha and his government. The police also have a say. The old-line bureaucracy battles against change; it delays and does manage to slow Botha's pursuit of reform. Aside from the party and the cabinet, however, it is obviously the military that is the leading decision-making institution in today's South Africa—both because of Botha's belief in its abilities and its clear-sightedness, and because he ascended to the top without other powerful connections.

Individuals from the Defence Force are at the core of the formal and informal dimensions of all South African policymaking. The influence of the military is increasing, even if South Africa is still a long way from becoming a jackboot state in the Latin American sense. There are important countervailing tendencies: The inertia of a bloated bureaucracy (including the parastatals) will tend to block South Africa's conversion to Prussian-style government. Yet Botha shares the military's vision of a fortress South Africa, tactically reformed but strategically sound if not hegemonic. The soldiers are his chosen instrument and he is theirs.

Notes

1. Quoted in Caryle Murphy, "South African Military Exerts Influence on Policy," *Washington Post,* 30 May 1980.

2. Quoted in Deon Geldenhuys, *South Africa's Search for Security Since the Second World War* (Johannesburg, 1973), 3.

3. See Hermann Giliomee, *Parting of the Ways: South African Politics 1976–1982* (Cape Town, 1982), x–xi.

4. Note, however, that because the instruction of military officers has been largely domestic since 1960, the world view of today's serving upper ranks is necessarily little influenced by overseas training or service. A B. Mil. from the Saldanha Bay Military Academy may not substitute adequately for a year at Sandhurst or Leavenworth.

5. Chester A. Crocker, *South Africa's Defense Posture: Coping with Vulnerability* (Beverly Hills, 1981), 85.

3

The Soviet Threat to Southern Africa

Robert Legvold

T here is no understanding Soviet policy and strategy in any region, including southern Africa, without understanding Soviet
foreign policy in general. And this cannot be understood without recognizing the Soviet Union's determination to be a global power,
entitled to a role wherever it deems its interests at stake, with the power
and influence to carry it off. It is also an alienated power. That is, Soviet
leaders reject many aspects of the existing international order: its structure of power (viewed as still too favorable to the West), its economic
hierarchy (viewed as still the creature of the industrialized market economies), its rules of play (viewed as still too favorable to U.S. technique),
and its obstacles to change (viewed as still too formidable to their friends
and favorites). Soviet leaders, Chernenko no less than Khrushchev, see
their country as the single most powerful force for rectifying these perceived deficiencies. This they do without dreaming of conquering or controlling the world. They seek influence, not real estate—not even others'
natural wealth.

The Soviet Union is also, for want of a better adjective, an ideological
power. Its perspective on the world differs fundamentally from that of
the United States, deriving as it does from a peculiar, often encrusted,
and highly institutionalized set of beliefs. Without suggesting that the
United States and its major allies are free of their own peculiar ideas, the
Soviet outlook means that every important area of change becomes for
East and West a contest of values as well as a test of strength. Cynical
the Soviet leaders are—but in superficial ways, not at the core of their
beliefs, and that is the problem.

This ambitious, alienated, and ideological power, however, exists in
a world as complex and intractable for itself as for others, a fact evident
to Soviet leaders. The reality of a fragmenting international order plagues
their policies as much as those of the West. The cohesion of Soviet alliances is as threatened as is that of the West, although in different ways.

Enemies are as immediate and powerful and, indeed, more numerous. Clients, particularly in the Third World, are as obstreperous and willful, and involvements with them as hazardous. Above all else, nuclear war casts as much of a shadow over Soviet policy as over that of the West, though popular myth in many Western circles has it otherwise.

As a result, Soviet policy faces an impressive and not always easily reconciled set of tasks. In order of importance, the Soviet priorities are first to secure the cohesion and stability of the Soviet domestic order by promoting an environment beyond Soviet borders that helps rather than hinders. Second, and by extension, the next most important policy task is to contribute to the endurance and viability of the Soviet alliance system in Eastern Europe. Third, policy must seek to avoid nuclear war. This belongs third because, as far as one can judge, Soviet leaders apparently would sacrifice it to the other two; they also, it seems, have a version of "better dead than (not) red," and events in Poland and the German Democratic Republic, not only in the Soviet Union itself, may trigger nuclear war.

Fourth, policy is expected to strengthen Soviet influence over developments, conflicts in particular, within regions bordering the Soviet Union. Whether Soviet leaders fancy themselves someday ruling over the critical strategic theaters ringing their own lands from northeast Asia through the Persian Gulf to the Balkans is impossible to tell. This belongs to the realm of daydreams, and Soviet leaders do not say much about their daydreams. Whether, short of this, they aim at a kind of *droit de regard* over military trends within neighboring regions—making themselves in effect the security manager for each area—also cannot be settled on the basis of the evidence. Soviet leaders, however, do make plain a determination to prevent any other power from retaining or amassing greater influence than theirs in these areas; to guarantee themselves a major role in dealing with change in these areas, particularly violent change; and to see to it that Soviet interests, as they choose to define them, will be respected.

Fifth, and only fifth, policy is designed to reinforce Soviet standing as a power apart, possessing the same authority as the United States, the same claim to deference from lesser powers, the same opportunity to mediate and therefore to influence international conflicts, and the same right to intervene in any quarter as Soviet leaders see fit. Crudely put, Soviet policy seeks to destroy the United States' double standard for the superpowers while preserving one for everyone else.

Sixth, and only sixth, the Soviet Union means to undergird the global reach of its power with facilities, friendships, and political access in the most far-flung regions. From Southeast Asia to Central America, from southern Africa to the Middle East, the Soviet Union wants more "coaling stations," parapets, and friends in high places. With them, it intends to protect its own expanding lines of communication, lanes of commerce, and vast fishing fleet; and, it should not be doubted, *in war* to threaten those of its major Western adversaries.

Soviet leaders, however, also view this infrastructure as vital to the seventh task of policy: promoting (and protecting) change in tune with their notions of a more desirable world. This comes last, not because it is unimportant to Soviet leaders, but because the other six are still more important. Unless, however, it is recognized that Soviet leaders are driven at some level by more than the desire to aggrandize Soviet power, a crucial policy impulse will be missed.

Only the last three of these objectives have much to do with most of the Third World and the dramas within. Soviet priorities, in short, not merely Soviet objectives, are important. Russia, Europe, and surrounding territories—not southern Africa—remain the point of departure for Soviet foreign policy. Moreover, when Soviet leaders address the problems closest and most critical to them, they do so directly, not vicariously with roundabout strategies for assailing nearby adversaries from afar. Soviet policy in southern Africa comes *after,* not as part of, Soviet policy in Europe and Asia.

True, the United States figures in all seven priorities, lending them a superficial unity. The only compelling threats to Soviet security and peace of mind, after all—at least the only consciously instigated ones—are those that Soviet leaders can imagine the United States raising or backing. The threat of China, for example, but for the shadow of U.S. complicity, would not be nearly so menacing. Neither the North Atlantic Treaty Organization nor Germany, but for the introduction of U.S. power, would occupy Soviet policymakers as they now do. Only the United States is the Soviet Union's fit partner and foe in shaping the nuclear threat. And only the United States sets the standard of superpower status—not to mention setting the widest range of obstacles to its achievement by the Soviet Union.

The United States also lurks in the background of nearly everything of concern to the Soviet Union in the Third World. If any political force can threaten or impede the growth of Soviet facilities and access in the Third World, it is the United States. If these facilities and access are intended to constrain and counter the power of any particular country, it is that of the United States. If any other country's successes and failures in the Third World affect the overall global balance, they are, again, those of the United States. If any other country can affect the pace and character of change nearly everywhere in the Third World, it is the United States. Finally, if any country symbolizes and leads history's alternative to socialism, it, too, is the United States.

Yet the Soviet preoccupation with the United States hardly means that Soviet policy in places like Southern Africa is not the product of a great many other considerations. Nor does it make these regions only battlegrounds in a U.S.-Soviet contest and nothing more. International politics is too complicated for that, and Soviet priorities are too disjoined. For Soviet leaders, only regions on Soviet borders—Europe, the Persian Gulf, northeast Asia—are strategic preoccupations; only they are approached with strategic criteria constantly uppermost; only they regularly make it onto the daily agendas of the men at the top. Areas beyond are regions of opportunity, attractive precisely because change does not automatically threaten the underlying East-West balance and Soviet advances do not inevitably risk provoking superpower confrontation. Granted that Soviet policymakers harbor a permanent urge to displace U.S. power almost everywhere (along with French, Chinese, Israeli, and Saudi power), nonetheless the urge has never become a compulsion. By the same token, gains in these areas are, from the Soviet perspective, worth fewer risks than Soviet stakes in the critical close-in theaters. If the superpowers come eyeball to eyeball again, it will not be over Nicaragua or Namibia, but over Iran or its equivalent. This is so because the Soviet leadership has no intention of accepting a head-to-head military conflict with the United States in Central America or southern Africa. It has no intention of doing this, not only because the military balance favors the United States in such cases, but because neither is central to the strategic contest between East and West as the Soviet Union conceives it.

This is not to say that, when Soviet leaders think about southern Africa, strategic considerations never cross their minds, or that the West's dependence on minerals from this area has no place in their calculations. On the contrary, nearly every Soviet piece of writing on the area alludes to the minerals. Some also refer to South Africa's position "at the junction of two oceans," giving the country "great strategic value to the West." Indeed, as this particular account concludes, "this is why it [South Africa] can be described as an extremely important bridgehead of world imperialism, whose loss would deal a telling blow to its own positions."[1] Rather, I am arguing that in the case of southern Africa these are second-level considerations, a matter for wartime planners, a pleasant vision were these resources already under Soviet command, but not a primary guide to policy—policy that in reality must respond to richer and more immediate pressures.

Soviet Policy in Africa South of the Sahara

The framework of Soviet policy in southern Africa is black Africa, not Europe. Understanding the twists and turns, aims and concerns, of Soviet policy below the Zambezi comes easier if one has some sense of the evolution of Soviet policy elsewhere on the continent. The Soviets, after all, have been engaged in this part of the world, struggling, hoping, learning, and plotting, for more than a quarter century. Much of that time their policy has been keyed to developments outside southern Africa.

Leaving aside prehistory—that is, Russia's eighteenth-century liaison with Abyssinia and the Comintern's desultory liaison with the South African Communist party from the 1920s—Africa became a serious, working object of Soviet foreign policy only after decolonization. Ghanaian independence in 1957 launched the Soviets in Africa. For the next decade Soviet policy surged and swelled from early naive expectation. Introduced to President Sékou Touré's seemingly radical regime in Guinée in 1958 and Patrice Lumumba's Congo (Zaire) a year later, and knowing little about the soil from which they grew, Soviet leaders took black Africa for a new revolutionary front. An exuberant General Secretary Nikita Khrushchev was at the helm; and his vision of newly independent states, in ever-increasing number revolting against Western tutelage and eventually Western political ways, went hand in hand with his other excesses: the year 1958 was one year after the launching of Sputnik and the first Soviet intercontinental ballistic missile (ICBM), the year the Soviet Union provoked the second great Berlin crisis, a move to highlight the shift in power under way. The next year was the year Khrushchev made his boast, later written into the 1961 Party Program, of catching and passing the mightiest capitalist economy within eleven years.

His transport had little to do with an overt, comprehensive Soviet strategy. Its inspiration was written into events. The Soviet Union would press the Western powers in central Europe, the fulcrum of the postwar world; the momentum of Soviet scientific and economic progress, coupled with the gathering force of defecting new nations, would do the rest. In Africa, the Soviet Union arrived and began choosing sides immediately. By 1960 African states were dividing over the Congolese conflict, the Algerian war, and relations with former colonial powers. Moscow did not merely side with the so-called Casablanca group (Algeria, Ghana, Guinée, Mali, Morocco, and the United Arab Republic) against the so-called Brazzaville (later Monrovian) group of "splitters" and "imperialism's collaborators"; it embraced the wave of the future. Its aid program, its insinuated partnership in international forums, its imperious political advice for building the new society—virtually every aspect of its demeanor—revealed Soviet expectations. Eventually the Soviet leadership—although in this case Khrushchev had less than full support from several of his colleagues—even persuaded itself that the most advanced of these states, a group labeled "revolutionary democracies," had escaped across the line into socialism or, more accurately, onto the "path of socialist construction." Apparently inspired by the Cuban model,

Khrushchev after 1963 pronounced a number of regimes—Algeria, Ghana, Mali, and the UAR—the genuine item, accepting their single-party systems as adequate substitutes for Communist parties and their versions of Marxism, sometimes Leninism, as close enough.

Soon after Khrushchev fell in 1964, so did Algeria's President Ben Bella, then Ghana's President Kwame Nkrumah, and then Mali's President Modibo Keita. Much of the Soviet Union's second decade in Africa, from the mid-1960s to the mid-1970s, was spent coming to terms with African realities. As Soviet experts and policymakers now recognized, the Ghanaian, Malian, and other African revolutions had turned out to be mock enterprises, shallow affairs—half-baked, undisciplined, and rushed. History's castoffs in the Ivory Coast, Senegal, Tunisia, and Zaire had more staying power. If there were a wave of the future, by 1967–1968 it seemed to be the African militaries, more and more of whom were pushing the politicians aside and assuming power themselves.

Over the next ten years, Soviet leaders set their sights more realistically, trimmed commitments—"We shall do the most for the cause of international revolution if we first build up our own Soviet society," they now said—and settled down to diversifying their relations with a wide array of African states, giving increasing attention to inherently significant countries like Nigeria and less to simply congenial ones.[2] They also lost interest in Africa.

In the mid-1970s the pendulum swung again, released by dramatic change in southern Africa. The sudden, unanticipated collapse of Portuguese colonialism in 1974 seemed in one fell swoop to alter the whole picture. Colonial salients now gave way not only to independent regimes but to revolutions. These in turn seemed sure to increase the pressures on Rhodesia and Namibia and, once these territories fell to black rule, on the Republic of South Africa itself. For the first time, developments in southern Africa had become, in Soviet eyes, the wheelhouse of change on the continent, rather than—as for so long—its tow.

Rarely does Soviet policy on any problem or in any region shift overnight, and it would be misleading to leave the impression here that this next stage in Soviet African policy began full blown the day after the Portuguese regime collapsed in Lisbon. It was neither so fulsome nor so abrupt as that. In fact, in the preceding year or two, Soviet observers had already begun to feel better about trends in Africa. The counterrevolutionary wave that they feared with the collapse of so-called progressive regimes, the rise of African militaries, and the daunting obstacles to development never materialized. Instead of a Thermidor, or, as Soviet commentators put it, the "Latin Americanization" of Africa, the continent had settled into an uneasy political stasis, with change here and there, some countries moving in one direction, some in another. Regimes like that of Ghana that had lost their way had not lost it completely, as a third generation of leaders learned from both the Nkrumah experience and the backlash to it. Regimes that proclaimed socialism as their goal—"scientific socialism," not, as the Soviets saw it, the bastardized African version—still cropped up. They emerged in Somalia, the Malagasy Republic, and Benin to go with the ones already in place in Congo-Brazzaville and Guinée. To the toned-down satisfaction of Soviet observers, Africa's progressives this time around appeared less given to so-called leftist excesses and false hopes. As approving Soviet writers noted, they were proceeding more sensibly with programs to nationalize private holdings, expand the state sector, develop agriculture, and build grassroots political organization. And they were unambiguous in their commitment to Marxism-Leninism, often spelling it out in their national constitutions.[3]

Then came the Portuguese revolution. In a relative instant it put southern Africa's future in a new light. Soviet leaders, who for nearly a decade had left Africa to Africanists, suddenly took note. Africa again became a region of promise, an area capable of producing a revolutionary pattern rather than merely the odd revolution. Soviet leaders were not reverting to old illusions. They had not forgotten the perishability of supposed African revolutions, nor had they unlearned twenty years' lessons in the frustrations Africa holds for outsiders who come with preconceived notions. From all appearances, however, they placed a special faith in the men and regimes coming to power in Ethiopia, Mozambique, and Angola. These were revolutions, as the Soviets judged them, made of stiffer stuff—in part because they were won in armed struggle, led by men who bore arms rather than pamphlets, and in part because they faced real and powerful external threats that would keep them from growing soft.

For five years, from 1974 to 1979, Soviet excitement mounted—and not blindly or unrealistically. Soviet leaders were not thinking of all of Africa when they contemplated the significance of developments in these three countries. They knew many parts of the continent would remain untouched. In southern Africa, however, Mozambique and Angola were only a first installment. There, they assumed, a process greater than any single country was fast approaching denouement. Out of it the area would emerge remade. Once there were progressive, maybe even revolutionary, regimes in Salisbury (Harare) and Windhoek as well as Luanda and Maputo, what they knew still to be the long, arduous issue of South Africa would at last become inescapable. History would have written another small but distinctive chapter. The West would not be the better for it. And the growing list of African states that Soviet analysts celebrated, ten states in the first rank, six in the second, would take on a new coloration.[4]

It was not to be—not, in any case, so smoothly as Soviet leaders had anticipated in 1975–1976. In Zimbabwe the process went awry or, if not awry, then its own way. Power there passed to black Africans perceived as progressive black Africans—not despite the West but, in the end, through the West's good offices. Afterward, Zimbabwe's new rulers hardly threw themselves into the struggle to liberate the remainder of southern Africa and hardly rushed to embrace their would-be Soviet benefactors. Namibia, too, disappointed Soviet expectations. By the early 1980s Soviet observers could tell that Namibian independence was not, as the French say, for tomorrow. Coupled with major new distractions elsewhere—in Afghanistan, in Poland, in the Middle East—not to mention the deterioration of U.S.-Soviet relations, southern Africa's cloudier future stilled Soviet enthusiasm. By the early 1980s Soviet leaders were again taking the long view; day-to-day African concerns, South Africa included, were once more in the hands of Africanists and other middle-level bureaucrats.

Soviet Policy in Southern Africa

The Soviet Union has not applied itself methodically to the problems and opportunities of southern Africa. Its contemporary involvement does not grow out of a long-term, carefully invested strategy tracing back to the start of the anticolonial struggle, let alone back to the Third Comintern Congress in 1921 and the first appearance of the South African Communist party. In a real sense, the beginning of Soviet policy in southern Africa is hardly a decade old, with 1974 as the divide. All the long years of public diplomacy and sloganeering for national liberation, all the aid channeled to the MPLA, the Front for the Liberation of Mozambique (FRELIMO), and later to the ANC and SWAPO, were part of a different era. Physically, strategically, and conceptually, the current Soviet position originated with Mozambique's and Angola's independence.

Their independence, when it came, caught the Soviet leaders by surprise. Like everyone else, they had no way of foretelling the Portuguese revolution and the effects it would unleash. As far as they were concerned, and much as they may have regretted it, on the eve of April 1974 the status quo in southern Africa looked roughly as stable to them as it did to the U.S. authors of National Security Situation Memorandum (NSSM) 39. Although they had every intention of keeping up the drumbeat of condemnation and every intention of continuing their support to anticolonial and antiapartheid groups, neither their commentary nor their actions suggest any inkling of what was about to happen. Indeed, after 1972 they had cut off aid to Agostinho Neto's MPLA, as they concentrated on the bickering within the party, only to resume aid hastily in 1974.

When the Soviet leadership suddenly awakened to the portent of far-reaching change, it did not move instantly or decisively, nor did it devise a whole strategy leading from Angola to Zimbabwe to Namibia. Soviet actions in the early confusion of the Angolan civil war were tentative and uncertain—hardly the determined moves of a leadership with its mind made up and its ultimate goal firmly set.[5] Such has been the character of Soviet policy in the region ever since.

Aside from wanting their friends, the MPLA in Angola and the Zimbabwe African People's Union (ZAPU) in Rhodesia, to share in power, Soviet policymakers gave no indication of aiming for a particular outcome, nor did they seem especially eager to meddle with their military power. In Angola, their first steps unfolded cautiously, even hesitantly. Arms were sent to the MPLA in increasing numbers by late 1974, a period of substantially expanded Chinese assistance to the Front for the National Liberation of Angola (FNLA). In January 1975, however, when, under Organization of African Unity (OAU) pressure, the three contending Angolan factions agreed to a coalition government come independence and to a shared arrangement for the period of transition, the Soviets backed the idea.[6] Throughout the spring, as the situation deteriorated and the fighting between the FNLA and MPLA increased—particularly by May when the FNLA seemed to be getting the better of it—Soviet public statements appealed for strong Portuguese action to head off a civil war.[7] The Soviet media also reaffirmed the importance of a coalition government and, on at least one occasion, criticized outside intervention from any quarter.[8]

As one looks back on the tangled set of moves, countermoves, and separate moves that followed, several aspects of Soviet behavior are striking. First, although clearly the Soviets wanted the MPLA to hold its own among the warring factions and planned to give it considerable military support, nothing suggests that a large-scale direct joint intervention with the Cubans was even contemplated until the last moment. Instead, the Soviet Union apparently calculated that, provided the MPLA's military position was not undermined, it would do fine in whatever political arrangement was finally made—all the more because the radical officers in the Portuguese Armed Forces Movement were expected to stack the deck in its favor. The Soviet Union, as it saw the situation, had no reason to get out front. Second, although the South African role does not account for the steady increase in Soviet military aid over the summer months or for the initial appearance of Cuban advisers in June, nearly two months before the first South African patrols crossed into Angola, the South African decision to become heavily involved in October does appear to have been a turning point in the Soviet leadership's own thinking. Within a week of South Africa's escalation, the air- and sea-lift of Cuban troops had begun (suggesting, of course, that contingency planning had been prepared weeks before). Third, throughout the Soviet-Cuban intervention, Soviet leaders kept a wary eye on others, particularly the United States, the OAU, and—until late summer 1975 when it pulled out—China. Even after the large-scale Soviet-Cuban military operation began, Soviet leaders appeared ready to retreat if the United States drew itself up and did something. Not until the Senate ruled this out on December 19 were Soviet leaders confident that they were home free.[9] Never, until the very end, was the die cast.

Taken as a whole, Soviet actions in Angola have implications important for understanding the broader thrust of Soviet policy in the region. First, there is every reason to believe that a determined counter-intervention by the United States (leaving aside its questionable wisdom on other grounds) would have reversed the Soviet decision. Second, there is even reason to believe that, had the United States made an issue of preserving the Alvor accords and of avoiding superpower intervention early on—indeed, had it focused on the issue at all in the context of U.S.-Soviet relations—the Soviets would have been responsive. That would have still left the Cubans, who, if Carlos Rafael Rodríguez is to be taken at his word, had committed themselves even before they knew the Soviets were on board, and who could have mounted some kind of an operation even without Soviet support. It would also have been no guarantee of a different outcome within Angola itself. It is, however, a critical piece of evidence suggesting that Soviet policy in the region is neither so single-minded, undeflectable, nor ambitious as many assume.

What Soviet behavior in Angola hinted, its behavior in Rhodesia demonstrated. Faced with major constraints, headed by the determination of the frontline states to recapture control over regional crises from the superpowers, Soviet policy relented.[10] Looked at from this distance, the more remarkable aspect of Soviet actions is not how much military assistance was given to ZAPU and its military arm—some of it doubtless outside the OAU framework—or how readily they embraced the notion of armed struggle. The more remarkable aspect is how docilely the Soviets let the frontline states control the state of play, how unopportunistic (or inept) they were in exploiting politics within the Patriotic Front, how feebly they resisted the Lancaster House settlement, and ultimately how little they did—indeed, wanted to do—to set their defeated clients against Robert Mugabe and his victorious Zimbabwe African National Union (ZANU) after the February 1980 elections.

True, events dealt the Soviets as allies the weaker of the contending factions and, true, this time the frontline states, the Western powers—foremost the British—and even the South Africans (in pushing Ian Smith toward a settlement of some kind) all closed, rather than opened, opportunities to them. This fact, however, does not gainsay either the resigned Soviet response or the impact that the whole experience has had on Soviet thinking about the region. Indeed, Soviet behavior in the Namibian case has since 1978 been almost identical to that in Zimbabwe. Grumbling, it has gone along with Security Council Resolution 435 and the role of the Contact Group in shepherding it.[11] It has accepted virtually the same rationalization by which it abstained in voting on the original (1977) U.K.-U.S. U.N. resolutions for a negotiated settlement in Rhodesia: The Africans wanted it. In this case, not only the frontline states favor a settlement within the guidelines of Resolution 435; but, as Soviet accounts note, SWAPO, too, has embraced the idea. Although Moscow has its reservations, it has made it plain that it will not act on them.[12]

This is one side of Soviet policy in the region, an important side if the Soviet challenge in southern Africa is to be understood accurately and insights derived for dealing more effectively with it. There are other sides as well. When in 1974 Soviet leaders made southern Africa the focus of their hopes and attention, they were also reentering Africa as a certain kind of benefactor—as the military patron of progressive change. Somewhere along the line they had given up pretending that they had an all-purpose, all-around role to play. Economic development, other than token contributions—gestures to reassure friends or to secure commodities—became the West's problem (and duty, as Soviet representatives to UNCTAD and other forums liked to stress).

The figures spoke for themselves. From 1975 to 1979, Soviet arms deliveries to sub-Saharan African governments totaled $3.3 billion, seventeen times their value in the decade 1961–1971.[13] Economic credits meanwhile fell from $492 million in 1961–1971 to $335 million in 1975–1979 (even though Soviet economic credits to the Third World in general rose steadily from $3.8 billion in 1955–1964 to $6.2 billion in 1965–1974 to $10.6 billion in 1975–1981).[14] In 1981 the Soviet Union signed $2 billion in arms sales contracts with sub-Saharan African governments, almost four times the economic assistance given to the area over the previous quarter century.[15] (Western economic aid to these states in 1981 was $6 billion.)

Moreover, these aggregate statistics failed to indicate, as David Albright has pointed out, the special place the Soviet Union came to occupy in the military efforts of a growing number of black African states, including Angola, Mozambique, and Ethiopia.[16] From 1975 to 1979, $500 million of Angola's $890 million arms purchases came from the Soviet

Union, $170 million of Mozambique's $240 million, and $1.5 billion of Ethiopia's $1.8 billion. (Western and multilateral agency economic assistance to Ethiopia over this period was $725 million, Soviet economic assistance $125 million; Western aid to Angola $131 million, Soviet $15 million; Western aid to Mozambique $350 million, Soviet $5 million.)[17]

These sums—and their effect would only be heightened by adding trade statistics and numbers of military advisers—represented both a plight and a conception. A plight because the Soviet Union lacked the resources to contribute more in other areas, or so Soviet leaders said and doubtless thought. Foreign Minister Andrei Gromyko often and pointedly explained to Third World audiences simply how little his country had to give. But a conception because Soviet leaders, having donned the mantle of a global power and built their military strength to a certain point, believed they should play a more direct and active role in defending so-called progressive forces in places like southern Africa. Sometimes, defending these forces meant helping them defeat opponents who stood in their way. Admiral Sergei Gorshkov, the father of the modern Soviet navy, from the early 1970s spoke of protecting the "national liberation struggle" and made this one of the rationales for a stronger navy. Others also, long before southern Africa exploded in change, began writing of the link between the Soviet Union's growing ability to intervene with force and the course of national liberation.[18] When the Angolan events broke, Soviet leaders were in a mood to get involved, albeit cautiously.

Returning to Africa as a military patron also represents both a commitment and an opportunity. The Soviets tend to see themselves, along with the Cubans and one or two of their East European allies, as the only force able and willing to provide substantial military aid to so-called national liberation groups. When these groups triumph, as in Angola and Mozambique, the commitment almost automatically transfers to aiding with their national security. Both as a matter of Soviet credibility in the Third World at large (the Soviets, too, to judge from some of the private rationalizations offered after the invasion of Afghanistan, have a fear of appearing weak if Third World clients can be intimidated or overthrown), and as entrée with new and insecure regimes, the Soviet Union takes on a share of their defense. Hence the warnings of the Soviet ambassador in Mozambique after the South African raid on ANC facilities in Matola in 1981 ("If our friends are attacked, we will have an appropriate answer") and then the visit to Mozambique ports by two Soviet warships.[19] Hence the direct warnings given to Pretoria first privately at the United Nations in November 1983, and then publicly in a TASS statement in January 1984 about South Africa's aggressive acts in Angola.

These are not open-ended commitments, nor are they evidence of a Brezhnev doctrine for Angola and Mozambique. Were either regime to begin unraveling internally, the Soviet Union would be unlikely to save it by direct military intervention. On the contrary, the Soviet Union has carefully tailored the kinds of arms that it supplies and has hedged its own direct role. Had it, as one sensible observer has noted, provided Mozambique with more sophisticated weapons or assumed a direct role in the counterinsurgency effort against the MNR in the months before the March 16, 1984 Accord of Nkomati, or had it ostentatiously taken a larger part in preparing Angolan defenses in 1983, as it is doing in Syria, that would have been another matter.[20] Even before the diplomatic developments in southern Africa in early 1984, however, the Soviets were in no hurry to escalate their military involvement, granted that Africans had placed their own limits on military ties.

The Soviet Union, however, is not militarily engaged in southern Africa out of generosity (although its leaders, like the leaders of other great powers with forces dispatched around the world, may think so). It is there because opportunity beckons and because, once there, to leave involves risks and implied losses. First is the chance to add to the complement of air strips, bunkering facilities, storage depots, and communications installations serving the Soviet Union's sprawling military establishment. Soviet leaders want these primarily to keep an eye on and to offset the global infrastructure of the U.S. and for waging general war, including its strategic nuclear component, and then to enhance the tools by which they, in descending order of priority, (1) protect their proliferating lines of communication and commerce; (2) checkmate the ability of the West, particularly the United States, to intervene with force, while in some instances mounting interventions of their own; and (3) intimidate local governments that get out of line (as the Ghanaians did in seizing Soviet fishermen in 1967) or bolster them with the visit of frigates or admirals when friends are in domestic trouble (as Somalia's President Siad Barre was in 1969 and 1970 and the Seychelles' President France Albert René was in 1981).

Second, the Soviets are eager to demonstrate that history is moving in the right direction, zigzags and all. Much of their definition of success and, indeed, much of their sense of legitimacy—the legitimacy of the so-called Soviet experience—rests on changes like those in Angola, Nicaragua, Yemen, and above all Vietnam—a fact driven home at every party congress and by every major foreign-policy speech in between. Trends alone, even if not much aided by the Soviets (as in Nicaragua or Mozambique) matter to them, reassure them, buoy them. If the Soviets have played a role, so easily and preeminently a military role, the effect is still more powerful.

Third, and often not so distinguishable from the second, Soviet leaders instinctively favor trends or events that diminish U.S. power and influence. On the surface, southern Africa has from the start appeared to the Soviets as a place where U.S. influence must inevitably dwindle. If by playing the role of military benefactor the Soviets can speed the process, most assuredly they will. The trick for them is always to work at the problem indirectly—to displace the Americans, not to defeat them. Defeating them is a high-risk proposition for which, in any event, in all but the most favorable circumstances the Soviet Union lacks adequate military power.

Because Soviet policy in southern Africa is the creature of all of these contending impulses, and not of any one of them alone—least of all the last—it is not accompanied by a coherent, well-honed strategy dedicated to a single objective. To believe the Soviet Union measures every step in accord with a consuming desire to capture the strategically valuable minerals in the region and thus to strangle Europe and, through Europe, the United States, requires incredible powers of simplification and what a psychologist would call a tendency for projection. No doubt Soviet leaders would welcome the leverage that control over the flow of minerals would yield—were it in fact as great as worst-case analysts fear. Nevertheless, there is literally no evidence in what they write, in what the more candid of them say privately, or in their actions to date to suggest that such a resource war is a conscious, first-order priority or practical guide to workaday policy.[21]

Soviet Policy toward South Africa

South Africa, as any Soviet policymaker or scholarly analyst knows, is the ultimate issue in southern Africa, maybe in all of Africa. Yet the Soviet Union really does not have a South African policy, much as it does not have an Israeli policy in the Middle East; it has only a policy toward a situation, accompanied by half a strategy. The situation comes in two parts: first, South Africa's internal evolution and the prospects for far-reaching change, and second—but invariably ahead of the fate of South Africa—the challenge raised by South Africa's counteroffensive within the region. These, of course, are mutually reinforcing, acutely so since 1974. What begins in the Soviet mind as an opportunity to affect the outcome in South Africa from neighboring states ends, at the moment, in the challenge raised by South Africa's determination to erase that opportunity and restore, through intimidation, a de facto cordon sanitaire. Added to this mix is the U.S. role, always a looming factor in Soviet calculations.

To begin where the Soviet leadership almost certainly does not—with the destruction of apartheid and the transformation of South African society: Neither drives Soviet policy. Not that Soviet leaders are insincere in their commitment to black rule in South Africa and, better yet, black rule with socialism—but, because the chances of either happening soon are slim (even in their view), policy focuses on more imminent issues. South Africa's revolution serves as a lodestar, it seems, rather than a constant, immediate source of policy. As a practical consequence, therefore, the Soviet strategy for South Africa is long-term and still basically evolutionary. Soviet leaders, following in effect the more expert judgment of the South African Communist party (SACP), in their most optimistic moments speak of "winning liberation" within the "lifetime of the present generation," but privately their specialists hold less hope.

South Africa is not Rhodesia, as Soviet observers know full well. Its social and political foundations are hardly about to crumble. Armed struggle will not soon carry the day; indeed, for this reason, Soviet analysts continue to assign it a subordinate and secondary role. Change, as they see it, will only come out of a long-term political struggle, designed to shrink what they call the social base of apartheid. South Africa's revolution is to be a fatal erosion by defection, with critical segments of the society turning their backs on the Afrikaners, rather than a gathering storm of revolutionary warriors overrunning the institutions of power. Soviet analysts count on a loose, multitiered process. At its base are the blacks—oppressed, disenfranchised, and presumably increasingly disaffected—and their youth in particular; then the Asians and Coloureds; then leaders of social and economic institutions, such as religious figures, who reject apartheid (Bishop Denis Hurley, president of the Catholic Bishops' Conference; Allan Boesak, president of the World Alliance of Reformed Churches; and Bishop Desmond Tutu, formerly the general secretary of the South African Council of Churches, are all mentioned), and business circles, who fear the effects of social conflict, including "influential foreign investors" and local business circles (for example, as noted in Soviet accounts, the National Development and Administration Fund, the Federated Chamber of Industries, and the Association of Chambers of Commerce). Finally, there are the liberal forces among the white population, who recognize the injustice and even more the impossibility of preserving institutionalized discrimination on such a scale—forces growing most rapidly, say the Soviets, again among the youth.

Inevitably these different segments of society and a host of organizations representing them may head in different directions, according to the Soviets, resisting the system in their own ways. The critical effect will be cumulative, however, be it the strengthening of black trade unions and the rise of civic protests against the growth of prices, rents, and the cost of transport services or the more timid unease of business leaders raising their voices against racial discrimination "as incompatible with economic growth." Students organizing, creating strike funds, and working with African trade unions are as much a part of the process as are young blacks fleeing their homeland and preparing themselves for the South African underground at Mazimbu or in the Angolan camps. Armed violence is treated as a galvanizing mechanism, a means to hearten blacks faced with the seemingly overwhelming power of the state, a fillip to less bold protestors, reinforcement for business interests worried about mounting disorder, and proof to the regime that its defenses are no longer unbreachable. The last is expected to pay even greater dividends, at a time when "contradictions are now rending the 'white tribe,'" when the National party has split and "seditious ideas have penetrated even racist institutions that only recently seemed immutable—the Dutch Reformed Church and even the Broederbond."[22]

The process, as Soviet observers apparently envisage it, is not so much the ascendancy of revolutionary violence toward some moment of truth as it is a synergism among the many forces at work within South African society, accelerated by armed struggle, hollowing out the underpinnings of the system until at some distant point it begins to crumble and change. The image of South Africa someday going up in revolutionary flames rarely, if ever, appears in Soviet analyses.

Moreover, despite the quickening of events since 1974, Soviet commentators apparently also recognize the many cross-currents at work within South African society, beginning with the attitude of the white worker. Though theoretically a natural ally, in fact white workers are, say Soviet sources, "infected with racial prejudice." The struggle "to clear their minds of the poisonous fumes of chauvinism," writes Yusuf Dadoo, chairman of the SACP, in the World Marxist Review, "will be long and hard."[23] Within the black community there is, thanks to the Bantustan policy, as Soviet authors acknowledge, a "stratum interested in the success of [the regime's] racist policy and ready to cooperate with it."[24] As the chiefs, the administrative elite, and "nascent African bourgeoisie" in the Bantustans can be bought off, so, admit Soviet authors, can some of the leaders of the Coloureds. Several Soviet sources have commented on the decision of Allan Hendrickse and David M. Curry to swing the support of the Labour party behind the constitutional reform of 1984.[25] Were these complications and a great many others like them not enough, one has to add, as do Soviet commentators, the problems of waging guerrilla warfare in a country without jungles; the timidity of neighboring states in the grip of South Africa's economic power or under the shadow of its military might; divisions within the OAU; the leverage that the South African regime has over its black population through the elaborate apartheid system; and ultimately the sheer strength of South Africa's army, police, and other instruments of control. Toppling the system from within—and Soviet commentators repeatedly underscore that the battle will have to be fought and won within South Africa—will not be easy.

Despite their belief in fighting and winning the battle within South Africa, however, Soviet leaders also see the context beyond South African borders as important, indeed, as the rear of the revolution. Since South Africa sees this as well, and has adopted a highly offensive strategy to deal with it, the Soviet Union's most immediate priority is to checkmate South African foreign policy, a task rather beyond its means.

The Soviets make no bones about the general sequence: "African countries," they maintain, have been effectively practicing "the tactics of 'selecting the weakest link' and advancing stage-by-stage to their ultimate objective of ending colonial rule."[26] First the French were defeated in Algeria; then, after a long struggle, the Portuguese in all their African colonies. "After that goal was accomplished, action was shifted to Zimbabwe and Namibia"—and now to Namibia and South Africa. Never mind this fairy-tale account of what Africa has been up to over the last twenty years; in this sequence, countries in South Africa's strategic rear—Angola, Mozambique, Zimbabwe, and Zambia—have a critical role to perform. Soviet leaders have been mindful of the hazards compelling these countries to play this role with great caution, but they have expected them to play it nonetheless and, in playing it, to alter the context of the South African struggle. Although the Soviets have not attempted to bully the leaderships of these countries into running larger risks than they dare, they have nonetheless hoped to inspire in them a measure of resolve. Their own military efforts in the region, including Soviet (and East European and Cuban) assistance to the ANC, are doubtless intended partly to stiffen the backbone of local leaderships.

No wonder, therefore, that the Soviet reaction to the Mozambique–South African nonaggression (Nkomati) pact has been so cool and even a little stunned. Soviet leaders had grown accustomed to South Africa's neighbors' treading a fine line. (Zimbabwe, good as its word, has since its independence in 1980 refused the ANC facilities, and the other countries bordering South Africa have sought to discourage the ANC from building anything resembling a military training base on their territories.)[27] But to cut a formal deal with Pretoria expressly at the ANC's expense!

True, the Soviet Union has been cautious itself, avoiding a precipitate and deep involvement. True, it assigns to many others roles ahead of its own. Take, for example, Angolan defense. When Soviet writers deal with the threats facing Angola, "fraternal assistance" from the socialist countries is never among the first items mentioned. In Veniamin Midtsev's hierarchy, Soviet aid comes fifth, after the restraining influence of Western nations such as France and West Germany, who are less quick than the Americans to excuse Pretoria; after the "unbending resolve of the leadership and the people of Angola to uphold the independence of their country;" after "the support from other Frontline States;" and after OAU solidarity.[28] That was never the order during the Vietnam War, and it is not today the order in the Middle East.

It is into this complicated lattice of attitudes and inclinations that the events of 1984 have intruded, minus one further important dimension. The background for Soviet leaders began three years earlier; 1981 is the watershed year. From that point, Soviet authors insist, the South African offensive took on a new character, as did the larger context in which it unfolded. The escalation of the military assault on the ANC beyond South African borders deep into Angola and against targets in Mozambique and Lesotho, as well as the expanded efforts to destabilize Angola, Zimbabwe, and Mozambique, Soviet authorities maintain, was largely a consequence of the shift in U.S. policy under President Reagan.[29]

We are thus brought back to a larger dimension of the problem. For most of the Carter years, the Soviet leadership paid scant attention to the interaction of U.S. and South African policies. Although it resented the U.S. role in mediating change in the region and disdained the efforts of Ambassadors Andrew Young and Donald McHenry as merely an attempt to salvage selfish U.S. interests, it also comfortably assumed that the United States would not do well with the new revolutionary regimes and that the U.S. rift with South Africa would only help, since the U.S. was not likely to go far enough to alter South African behavior or far enough to satisfy the African states, but only far enough to undermine any prospect of U.S.–South African collaboration. Under President Ford, Soviet leaders were actually eager to divorce southern African developments from U.S.-Soviet relations. Whatever they thought of the gambit implicit in NSSM 39 and then the flip-flop and sudden energizing of U.S. diplomacy in the region in 1976, their overriding interest was in decoupling Angolan developments from East-West détente. They were not about to make an issue of U.S. policy in the area while attempting to fend off Secretary of State Henry Kissinger's efforts to contest their own.

The situation now, however, is quite the reverse. The interconnection of U.S. and South African policies is again of importance to the Soviet leadership. President Reagan's alleged global offensive and South Africa's 1981–1983 regional offensive, they insist and no doubt believe, flow together. Part of Soviet strategy, of course, is to persuade the remainder of Africa, to the degree it needs persuading, that an unholy alliance has been struck between the two countries. Every measure of economic assistance (the 1982 $1.1 billion International Monetary Fund loan), every step toward military cooperation (easing restrictions on the sale of military-strategic goods) or cryptomilitary cooperation (lifting the ban on exports of nuclear-power equipment and plutonium-3), every U.S. Security Council veto protecting South Africa, and every visit of one country's intelligence or military officials to the other are picked up and trumpeted in Soviet accounts.[30]

Where previously U.S. and South African leaders were said to have only partly overlapping interests and divergent tactics, according to Soviet analysis, the contrast has been wiped away since 1981. Now the two countries are said to be on the same wavelength, pursuing largely identical objectives by complementary means. The Americans, they say, seek to preserve, "though not without some facelifting," a South African regime "that would be a reliable ally"; to "suppress or to disorganize the national liberation movement in South Africa"; to stall in Namibia while "fostering pro-Western forces there capable of counteracting SWAPO"; to "destabilize the countries of socialist orientation in the region" while "dragging them into various talks at which it is difficult to discern the carrot from the stick"; to "undermine the group of Front-line States"; and, "last but not least, to guarantee for American corporations unimpeded access to the region's raw materials."[31] With U.S. objectives phrased in this way, there is little with which the Soviets would think the South African government disagrees.

Soviet leaders have reacted to this alleged intriguing with a mixture of smugness, distress, and defiance. On the one hand, despite a growing frustration and anger over U.S. policy in general, their pose has been to downplay its effectiveness and, by extension, the potency of the United States' supposed alliance with South Africa. Thus, despite the sweeping aims attributed to the Reagan administration, the malevolence of its attitude toward the Soviet Union and its friends, and the inflexibility of its policy, Soviet leaders insist that Washington's accomplishments are few and puny. Such, at least, has been one face put on the challenge of the Reagan administration.

At the same time, however, Moscow let U.S.-Soviet relations sink to a level unseen since the worst moments of the Cold War; indulged an exceptional degree of suspicion and hostility; and adopted a harsh, inflexible, and aloof strategy in response. Over the autumn months of 1983, with the collapse of the intermediate-range nuclear missile force (INF) negotiations in Geneva, the U.S. invasion of Grenada and escalating pressures on Nicaragua, and mounting instability in the Middle East, many Soviets even began glumly and with considerable alarm to talk about a complete collapse of the restraining framework of arms control and the renewed risk of direct confrontation between the superpowers.

Two separate concerns had merged to push Soviet leaders beyond their earlier defiant equanimity to a new level of apprehension: First, largely because of their view of the Reagan administration's behavior in the area of arms control, in particular its handling of the Soviet walkout from the INF talks, Soviet leaders had become convinced that the administration did not take the Soviet Union seriously; that it believed the Soviet leadership had merely been playing games; and that it failed to understand the peril now facing the entire edifice of arms control, including the Strategic Arms Reduction Talks (START). (Rather than yielding on the issue of their own missiles in Europe, the Soviets, if and when they returned to START, would surely simply add the American Pershing IIs and ground-launched cruise missiles to the bill, making as they were aware, the Soviet proposal still more nonnegotiable in U.S. eyes. START, they sensed, was about to become moribund.) Second, U.S. actions in the Caribbean and Central America, together with its use of military force in the Middle East, had apparently persuaded Soviet leaders that the administration was not nearly so passive as its moderate U.S. friends claimed. Soviet analysts were not suggesting that Reagan and his people wanted a confrontation with the Soviet Union or, for that matter, a test of U.S. strength in the Middle East. But they were beginning to worry about what the administration might stumble into, particularly when, as they judged from its actions in Central America, its disposition had grown self-confident and assertive. For all the Soviet leadership's distractions, they knew that there were circumstances from which their leadership, too, would not retreat.

When suddenly the South African diplomatic breakthroughs of February and March 1984 burst on a startled world—and no leadership, from all appearances, was more startled than the Soviet Union's—this was its general frame of mind. It remains the psychological context within which Soviet observers attempt to understand the Lusaka and Nkomati accords and to anticipate their consequences.

Soviet leaders and those who advise them, not surprisingly, have scarcely been delighted by this development. Viewed through Soviet eyes, both agreements reflect the weaknesses of their allies and a fundamental vulnerability to South African power that they either could not or would not attempt to offset with Soviet assistance. Both vindicate, at least in the short run, South Africa's brutal, aggressive forward strategy of the past few years. Both, as Soviet observers well know, are seen by the Reagan administration (and many of its nonplussed critics) as a major success for its policy. Small wonder, therefore, that public Soviet comment has been so strained. Not wanting to criticize their friends openly, Soviet press accounts have been conspicuously thin, offering only a hint of unhappiness. One of the ablest of Soviet Africanists, for example, has observed that South Africa's policy "of military blows and economic blackmail," together with "proposals for talks and various kinds of agreements wears down the weak African states and misleads world public opinion."[32] Another well-placed authority murmured in a piece published before the signing of the March 16, 1984, accord that "strong-arm methods . . . hardly make for durable understandings, especially when the groundwork for them is shaky," and went on to contrast the purposes of Mozambique and Angola in negotiating with South Africa (to seek an end to Pretoria's aggression in the region) with those of South Africa and the United States (to "perpetuate the apartheid system, put an end to the international isolation of the racist regime, and strengthen the positions of Western powers and South Africa in Namibia by installing a puppet government in Windhoek").[33] It takes little imagination to see which parties he thought would come closer to achieving their ends.

In private one could get a somewhat fuller sense of the Soviet reaction. Soviet policymakers, it turned out, though enamored of neither agreement, regarded the Accord of Nkomati as the more unfortunate.[34] The Lusaka agreement on the disengagement of South African troops from southern Angola inspired little enthusiasm but evoked less concern. Few seemed to believe that it would seriously jeopardize SWAPO's struggle; even fewer saw it as a first step toward a Namibian settlement linked to the withdrawal of Cuban forces.[35] (On the contrary, more than once Soviet speakers pointed to the March 19 Angolan-Cuban communiqué tying for the first time the Cuban presence to the internal threat to the MPLA.) No one seemed to fear or even to be conscious of the possibility that Luanda's readiness to deal with Pretoria portended, as one thoughtful U.S. specialist believed, that "the MPLA, weakened by South Africa and UNITA, economically starved by the Soviets and their own misman-agement, and persuaded that recognition by the United States would mean economic assistance, became prepared in 1985 to diminish its reliance on the Soviet Union and chance some kind of merger with or absorption by UNITA."[36] A few Soviet observers even granted that, on balance, the agreement might work to Angola's advantage if it turned out to ease the military pressures on the regime.

Nkomati, however, was discussed differently. Nkomati betrayed long-standing African principles. Nkomati accepted terms that before had always been rejected by African leaderships. Nkomati, as one man put it, enshrined peaceful coexistence defined according to South African preferences. Nkomati, although no one uttered the words, was struck on the backs of people who deserved better. As one might expect of an agreement negotiated from weakness, according to the Soviet view, the deal had left the better cards in South Africa's hands.

Even in private, however, Soviet speakers refused to translate their obvious distaste for the March 16 agreement into criticism of President

Samora Machel and his colleagues. The act, not the actors, was condemned, an awkward but determined piece of footwork. Indeed, within weeks of the ceremony at Nkomati, *Pravda* carried a long, sympathetic two-part article on Mozambique, as if to reaffirm the Soviet Union's support for its leadership.[37] The three authors, senior figures who traveled to Mozambique at the invitation of FRELIMO's central committee, wrote enthusiastically of the country's struggle, against great odds, to build a new society according to "socialist ideals." When the Nkomati accord was introduced—other than to note how desperately Mozambique needed relief—it was to highlight the political and ideological gap that, they had been assured, still divided this "revolutionary" society from the other camps.[38] It was also to quote Mozambiquan sources who swore continued devotion to the war against apartheid.

Soviet coyness in this instance appeared to be more than putting a brave face on a bad situation. Rather, it had to do with a more basic calculation. Although one cannot be sure how widely and confidently shared the sentiment is among Soviet leaders and analysts, a number of them voiced the conviction that the accords of 1984 would never last. Because they believe so deeply in the cynicism of the South African leadership and, therefore, in the unlikelihood of further agreements in the region—and because they also believe that the situation, unless it advances, will relapse—any stabilization between South Africa and its radical neighbors, in their view, has a short life to live. Several of them spoke of the inherent vulnerability of the Nkomati and Lusaka accords: Even were the two sides likely to act in utter good faith, the near impossibility of controlling headstrong third parties guarantees, in their judgment, continued violence, which sooner or later will provoke retaliation by one side or the other. In short, until Soviet biases are shaken by a Namibian settlement, their longer-term faith in the fragility of any modus vivendi, struck as this one had been, will preserve their peace of mind.

Meanwhile, they continue to look at South Africa and relations within the region through the fog of their bitter relationship with the Americans. Until this begins to lift—which is not likely to happen soon under a reelected Reagan administration—the Soviet leadership will not be capable of finding nuance and progress in South Africa's foreign policy or of expecting good to come from the fragile, uncertain diplomatic process under way. On the contrary, the emphasis will be on the perils of political settlements offered by Pretoria and engineered by Washington. The preoccupation will be with the joint treachery of those who, according to Soviet slogans, seek hegemony in the region in league with those who seek it everywhere else.

For the moment, the Soviet role has shrunk still further, even in Angola and Mozambique. Nonetheless, Soviet leaders are not likely to act dramatically or desperately to undo the loss—short of an imminent reversal of alliances by Maputo or Luanda. Even then, for want of real options, it is not inconceivable that the Soviet response would be relatively weak. General Secretary Konstantin Chernenko and his colleagues cannot be happy, but in all likelihood their course will be as before: Since abandoning the inflated expectations of 1974–1979, Moscow has pressed forward with diplomatic, military, and party ties with Angola and Mozambique and, where possible, with Zimbabwe, a country in which the Soviet Union expects to do considerably better over the next few years. It has also contributed modestly but steadily to the defense of Angola and Mozambique, a role whose cachet may have been reduced, but not eliminated, by the February and March accords. And it has assumed a large part in supplying and training the ANC, perhaps a part now to be expanded. Of course, it has also made an intensive effort to exploit the Reagan administration's policy of so-called constructive engagement with South Africa and its apparent backsliding on the Namibian question.[39] An enormous propaganda campaign has been under way—reinforced, one can be sure, by what Soviet policymakers say in private to African leaders—to drive home the significance of Washington's alleged alliance with South Africa.

Moreover, broader foreign-policy considerations, including an increasingly surly attitude toward the Americans and a tendency to read transcendent significance into regional developments, add to the inflection of policy. Beyond the desire to improve their own position in southern Africa or to do harm to that of the West, in the circumstance, Soviet leaders are constantly tempted to prove their mettle, to expose the folly of hard-line Western policies, to convince third parties of their own toughness, and to show U.S. clients, such as they assume South Africa to be, that a more assertive United States does not guarantee them more freedom of maneuver. Southern Africa is not likely to be the place where the Soviet Union settles scores with the Reagan administration or chooses to face down the United States. A mood of special testiness and antagonism exists, however, albeit for the moment without an easy mode of expression in southern Africa, and it is likely to linger for some time.

If the accords of 1984 fray and snap and the region again collapses into violence, as many Soviet analysts expect, then the Soviet Union— sour mood and all—is likely to reenter the picture quickly. Not that its reentry need be marked by recklessness. The Soviet leadership has not grown more impetuous or incautious, but its overall state of mind will hardly soften its natural competitiveness and eager opportunism. Beleaguered allies are likely to find it a willing source of military support, at least until that point when the specter of superpower confrontation intervenes (and provided that it does).

If, on the other hand, the uneasy and incomplete peace of the moment lasts longer than Moscow expects, Soviet leaders are hardly likely to write the region off. Their faith has always been in a situation—far more than in today's clients or in this moment's opportunities. So long as the underlying problems at the root of South Africa and southern Africa's tensions persist, they will continue to believe in the future. Africa will again have taught them its tortuous ways, but they are a patient lot.

Notes

1. A. Runov, "South Africa: Citadel of Racism and Reaction," *International Affairs,* 11 (November 1976), 72.

2. Not that Moscow for the first time approached Africa's more moderate regimes. From 1962–1963, when relations were established with Senegal, Nigeria, and Kenya, the Soviet Union had actively sought expanded ties.

3. See E. Melnikov, "Politicheskie preobrazovaniya v Afrikanskikh stranakh sotsialisticheskoi orientatsii" (Political transformations in African states of a socialist orientation), *Mirovaya ekonomika i mezhdunarodnye otnosheniya,* 12 (December 1981), 121. For a fuller and enthusiastic discussion of the notion of African states of "a socialist orientation," giving the concept the patina of theoretical importance, see Anatoly Gromyko, *Afrika: Progress, trudnosti i perspektivy* (Africa: Progress, Problems, and Prospects) (Moscow, 1981), 75–97.

4. By the late 1970s Soviet commentators grouped Algeria, Angola, Benin, Ethiopia, Guinée, Congo, Libya, Madagascar, Mozambique, and Tanzania in a category of states making "far-reaching economic and social changes . . . facilitating and accelerating their possible transition to socialism" (a tame version of the 1963–1964 formulation). A second cluster of states—Guinea-Bissau, the Cape Verde Islands, São Tomé and Principe, Seychelles, Mali, and Zimbabwe—were said to be taking constructive but less advanced steps. See, for example, Gleb Starushenko, "Chosen Path," *New Times,* 40 (October 1980), 18. Starushenko is a deputy director of the African Institute.

5. There are a number of useful commentaries on the Soviet role in the Angolan War, including Jiri Valenta, "Soviet Decision-Making on the Intervention in Angola," in David E. Albright (ed.), *Communism in Africa* (Bloomington, 1980), 87–117, as well as his "The Soviet-Cuban Intervention in Angola," *Studies in Comparative Communism,* XI (1978); Arthur Jay Klinghoffer, *The Angolan War: A Study in Soviet Policy in the Third World* (Boulder, 1980); Colin Legum, "Angola and the Horn of Africa," in Stephen S. Kaplan et al., *Mailed Fist, Velvet Glove: Soviet Armed Forces as a Political Instrument* (Washington, 1979); Peter Vanneman and Martin James, "The Soviet Intervention in Angola: Intentions and Implication," *Strategic Review,* IV (1976). The most balanced and incisive account is in Larry C. Napper, "The African Terrain and U.S.-Soviet Conflict in Angola and Rhodesia," in Alexander L. George (ed.), *Managing U.S.-Soviet Rivalry* (Boulder, 1983), 155–185.

6. See, for example, *Pravda,* February 16, 1975, 5. In contrast, the Americans did not publicly endorse the notion of a coalition government until summer 1975—too late.

7. See Napper, "The African Terrain," 160.

8. *Izvestiya* (May 21, 1975).

9. True, weeks before the passage of the Clark amendment, with the rout-

ing of Holden Roberto's forces in the north in early November, the tide of battle had turned in the MPLA's favor. The concern over a U.S. role, however, apparently lingered.

10. Not only did the five frontline states (Tanzania, Zambia, Mozambique, Botswana, and Angola) push ZAPU and ZANU into collaborating in the Patriotic Front and take the lead in managing the diplomacy among all key parties, including the British and the Americans, they also saw to it that all, or nearly all, arms to ZAPU and ZANU were channeled through the OAU Liberation Committee as well as determining what kinds of weapons could be introduced into the conflict. They did all of this because, as President Kenneth Kaunda of Zambia had said, "Our failure to find a solution here [in Angola] confirms that the Organization of African Unity has no power to shape the destiny of Africa. Power is in the hands of the superpowers, to whom we are handing Africa by our failure." Napper, "The African Terrain," 165, citing Colin Legum, "Foreign Intervention in Angola," Legum (ed.), *Africa Contemporary Record: Annual Survey and Documents, 1975–76* (London, 1976), A–1.

11. For Soviet reservations about Resolution 435 and a frank indication of the disadvantages that they believe SWAPO has suffered in this process, see A. Yu. Urnov, "Nechestivyi soyuz Vashingtona i Pretorii," (The Unholy Alliance of Washington and Pretoria) in *Belyi dom i chernyi kontinent* (The White House and the Black Continent) (Moscow, 1984), 75–80. Urnov is a senior policymaker. For a general account of the Namibian situation, see Yu.I. Gorbunov and A.V. Pritvorov, *Namibiya: problemy dostizheniya nezavisimosti* (Namibia, The Problems of Achieving Independence) (Moscow, 1983).

12. See Veniamin Midtsev, "Abetting the Racists," *New Times*, 45 (November 1979), 23–24. Significantly, Midtsev is a senior Africanist in the International Department of the CPSU's central committee.

13. David E. Albright, *The USSR and Sub-Saharan Africa in the 1980s* (Washington, D.C., 1983), 7. In neither case do these totals include assistance to so-called national liberation movements.

14. The first statistics, adjusted by the author to exclude North African countries, are from *Soviet Economic Prospects for the 1970s*, Joint Economic Committee of the U.S. Congress (Washington, 1973), 768; the second from Albright, *The USSR and Sub-Saharan Africa*, 95.

15. *Background Brief*, The Foreign and Commonwealth Office (London), July 1983. David Albright notes that the Soviet Union's annual average military sales to Africa have since dropped (from about $2 billion to $1.2 billion), while its economic assistance has increased. The imbalance between military and economic assistance, however, has not been altered in any essential way. See David E. Albright, "New Trends in Soviet Policy Toward Africa," *CSIS Africa Notes*, 27 (April 29, 1984), 8.

16. Albright, *The USSR and Sub-Saharan Africa*, 16. By 1975–1979 Albright reports that seventeen African countries were primarily dependent on the Soviet Union for arms supplies, four of them exclusively dependent (8).

17. In Albright's more recent study, he indicates that Soviet aid commitments to Mozambique have jumped from $5 million (1975–1979) to $100 million (for the 1980s); and to Angola from $15 million to $400 million. See Albright, "New Trends in Soviet Policy Toward Africa,"8.

18. The best illustration was V.M. Kulish (ed.), *Voennaya sila i mezhdu-*

narodnye otnosheniya (Military Force and International Relations) (Moscow, 1972), particularly the chapters written by A.M. Dudin and Yu.N. Listvinov.

19. *Le Monde* (March 20, 1981).

20. Seth Singleton, "The Shared Tactical Goals of South Africa and the Soviet Union," *CSIS Africa Notes*, 12 (April 26, 1983), 3.

21. I will not belabor the point here because I have had my say on this subject in congressional testimony and in "The Strategic Implications of the Soviet Union's Nonfuel Mineral Resource Policy," *The Journal of Resource Management and Technology*, XII (1983), 47–55. Frankly, what one believes on this score depends more on how one understands the basic character of Soviet foreign policy than it does on the issue itself. If one believes with James Arnold Miller that Brezhnev "at a secret meeting of Warsaw Pact leaders in Prague in 1973" said "that the Soviet objective was world dominance by the year 1985, and that the control of Europe's sources of energy and nonfuel minerals would reduce it to the condition of a hostage to Moscow," or if one believes that "as recently as [also] 1973 Leonid Brezhnev is reported to have told President Barre of Somalia [also] in Prague: 'Our aim is to gain control of the two great treasure houses on which the West depends, the energy treasure house of the Persian Gulf and the mineral treasure house of central and southern Africa,' " then elaborate analyses of Soviet foreign policy probably do not much matter. Nor, for that matter, does the fact that Barre was not in Prague in 1973. The Miller quote is from "Alarm: Alert Letter on the Availability of Raw Materials," mimeo., 54 (September 1983), 3. The second quote is from Richard Nixon, *The Real War* (New York, 1981), 25 (without a citation), and is repeated by Ambassador Donald B. Sole in an *Africa Report* interview (September–October 1981), 14–19.

22. Boris Asoyan, "Split in the 'White Tribe,' " *New Times*, 19 (May 1982), 22. At the time Asoyan was a correspondent in Africa. He is now a deputy director of the African Institute in Moscow.

23. Yusuf Dadoo, "Crisis of the Racist System in the South of Africa," *World Marxist Review*, 12 (December 1982), 19.

24. Runov, "South Africa," 67–68.

25. See, for example, L. Skuratov, "Racist Strategem," *New Times*, 13 (March 1983), 22–23.

26. Anatoly Gromyko (ed.), *Vneshnyaya politika stran Afriki* (The Foreign Policy of African Countries) (Moscow, 1981), 93.

27. Soviet public commentary had little to say about Zimbabwe's restraint; the reluctance of Mozambique and Zambia to give the ANC all that it might want was acknowledged in Soviet analyses, and, for the record at least, accepted.

28. Veniamin Midtsev, "Explosive Situation," *New Times*, 34 (August 1982), 9–10.

29. Presumably Soviet analysts know that the proximate cause was the increase in ANC sabotage—in particular the successful attack on South Africa's oil from coal plant in mid-1980; but, at the same time, Soviet leaders are doubtless convinced that Reagan's policy is the decisive factor.

30. See, for example, Y. Tarabrin, "U.S. Expansionist Policy in Africa, *In-*

ternational Affairs, 10 (October 1983), 41–50, and his "Afrika v globalnoi strategii imperializma" (Africa in the Global Strategy of Imperialism), *Mirovaya ekonomika i mezhdunarodnye otnosheniya,* 2 (February 1982), 25–37. Tarabrin is the head of the international relations department of the African Institute. See also A.Yu. Urnov, "Alyans Vashington-Pretoriya i Afrika" (The Washington-Pretoria Alliance and Africa), *Mirovaya ekonomika i mezhdunarodnye otnosheniya,* 3 (March 1982), 46–58. Urnov is the senior policymaker cited earlier.

31. Tarabrin, "U.S. Expansionist Policy in Africa," 42.

32. Boris Asoyan, *Southern Africa: Who is Sowing Dragon's Teeth* (Moscow, 1984), 45.

33. V. Midtsev, " 'Peacemaking' Masquerade," *New Times,* 12 (March 1984), 12.

34. Based on conversations in Moscow in April 1984 with both academic analysts and policymakers.

35. On the other hand, it was striking how insistent Soviet speakers had suddenly become on preserving and implementing Resolution 435, an undertaking that, as I indicated earlier, had never inspired much Soviet enthusiasm.

36. Robert I. Rotberg, "South Africa and the Soviet Union," below, 64.

37. See E. Grigorev, A. Serbin, and I. Tarutin, *Pravda,* April 23, 30, 1984.

38. In the second of these two articles, Machel is quoted as saying of the agreement: "There can be no question of our coexistence [with South Africa] in the sphere of ideology. We are different from one another. Our systems are antagonistic. We are for socialism and against capitalism."

39. On the last, beyond a constant stream of commentary in the central press, see V.Yu. Vasilkov, "Problema Namibii i Positsiya SShA" (The Namibian Problem and the Position of the U.S.A.), *SShA: Ekonomika, politika, ideologiya,* 4 (April 1983), 49–52.

4

South Africa and the Soviet Union: A Struggle for Primacy

Robert I. Rotberg

I n much of black Africa the Soviet Union struggles to rekindle the enthusiasm for Soviet-African cooperation that was so much a part of the continent's heady first years of independence. When Kwame Nkrumah was Ghana's president in the early 1960s and newly emerged Africa was ebullient, prosperous, and confident, Nkrumah set its ideological tempo and orchestrated much of its experimentation with the rhetoric and deeds of Marxism and socialism. Nkrumah listened to Soviet advisers; Moscow's emissaries had an influence that has been characterized as stronger and more persuasive than that of Nkrumah's own ministers and officials.[1] Even earlier the Soviets had been active and powerful in Guinée. Replacing the French, they had assisted President Sékou Touré and, snowplows or not, helped shape the policies of his nascent government. During Nkrumah's heyday and after, they were active in Mali, in revolutionary Zaire before the conclusive rise of General Joseph Mobutu, in Congo, in Madagascar, and to a lesser extent in Tanzania. The Soviet Union backed Idi Amin's reign of terror in Uganda, dabbled in the Sudan with only limited success, and attained dramatic recognition of their importance to Africa in the mid-1970s when the collapse of imperial Portugal led to the victory of Soviet-backed liberation movements in Guinea-Bissau, Saõ Tomé and Príncipe, Mozambique, and Angola.

No intervention was more salient than the Soviet Union's decision (buttressed by the refusal of the United States to intervene effectively)[2] to give massive assistance to the MPLA during the civil war of 1975 in Angola. After the failure of many well-meaning, African-supported attempts to forge a lasting political coalition among the MPLA, UNITA, and the Front for the National Liberation of Angola (FNLA), and the strong but ill-timed and self-defeating intervention of South African forces, the Soviet Union and its Cuban allies transformed a weak MPLA into the strongest of the three contending insurgencies and turned the tide of battle in its favor. Nowhere before in Africa had the Soviets used military might so openly. The Soviets spent about $500 million to install the MPLA in power; they supplied weapons and other materiel, transported Cubans, gave aircraft, and maintained a naval squadron off Luanda. They had trained armies and formed praetorian guards for Nkrumah and many others; in Angola, the victory of the MPLA was unquestionably acknowledged to be primarily a Soviet-Cuban conquest.

With their prestige increased and their ability to deliver a military punch now unquestioned, the Soviets moved beyond optimism to a policy that for the first time could have been called hegemonic. Powerful in all the Portuguese-speaking ex-colonies, in Uganda, and in Congo, and vigorous in Madagascar, they took advantage of the changing currents of politics in southern Africa to upgrade their support for the South West Africa People's Organization (SWAPO), for the African National Congress (ANC) (after the Soweto rising of 1976), and for Joshua Nkomo's Zimbabwe African People's Union (ZAPU). Active for some years in Somalia, where they had access to the valuable base and port of Berbera on the Gulf of Aden, they also attempted to curry favor with the ruling clique in revolutionary Ethiopia. The Somalis, intent on invading the Ogaden, in 1977 ousted the Soviets in the manner of Egypt and tried to gain Western backing for the war with Ethiopia of that year. The Soviets, entranced by the prospect of influencing the course of the already radical Ethiopian revolution and of trading a dominant role in a country of 35 million people for one in a country of only 4 million, airlifted weapons and heavy equipment to Addis Ababa. Without this urgent Soviet assistance, the stronger Somali army might have prevailed. With an infusion of critical materiel, however, and about 15,000 Cuban soldiers and a few thousand Soviet and East German advisers, the tide of battle was turned. In 1978 a Soviet general masterminded a desert offensive that, thanks largely to the Cuban troops, pushed the Somali army out of the Ogaden. To the triumph of Angola, the Soviets (again with Cuban help) had added the apotheosis of the Horn of Africa.

Admittedly, the Soviets in 1978 had backed a Cuban/Angolan thrust in the Shaba province of Zaire. That thrust, however, was repulsed by the West—particularly by French, Belgian, and Moroccan troops assisted logistically by the United States. The Soviets faltered, too, in Zimbabwe, when the end of the war and the nation's first election gave Robert Mugabe's Zimbabwe African National Union (ZANU), rather than Nkomo's ZAPU, decisive power. After Mugabe formed a government, Soviet ambitions were negated and ZAPU progressively weakened. Tanzania's invasion of Uganda in 1979 also ended Soviet and Libyan influence at the head of the Nile. A coup in Equatorial Guinea, also in 1979, ousted Francisco Macias Nguema, another dictator with Soviet ties.

There were advances, too, if less formative and significant than those in Angola and Ethiopia. In 1969 the Congo became officially Marxist-Leninist. Benin became another Marxist-Leninist government in 1974. Angola and Mozambique proclaimed themselves Marxist-Leninist states in 1978. So did Guinea-Bissau, São Tomé and Príncipe, Ethiopia, and Madagascar. Several governments of Ghana, brought to power by coups, leaned toward the Soviet Union. A Tanzanian-backed coup in the Seychelles in 1977 installed a radical socialist government in office. It accepted massive shipments of arms from the Soviet Union, welcomed Soviet naval vessels, sought economic assistance, received a large Soviet technical and diplomatic presence, and swerved left in policy as well as rhetoric.

By the end of the 1970s the Soviet position in Africa was decisive in Angola and Ethiopia, critical in countries like the Seychelles and Mozambique, strong elsewhere, and influential even in still Western-oriented nations like Zambia. Overall, despite what the Africans knew to be a disappointing record of economic aid, systematic interference with the sovereignty of the governments to which it was allied, hesitancy in the liberationist theater of southern Africa, and an uncertain reputation for true friendship and commitment, the Soviet Union had recovered from the disappointments of the late 1960s and early 1970s. Its counsel was appreciated, its power feared, and its influence throughout the continent impossible to ignore.

African clients nevertheless soon discovered that fundamental Soviet interests only occasionally coincided with the different self-interests of the individal weak, fragile nations. This was noticeably so in Ethiopia, where the government of Mengistu Haile Mariam was intent (as Emperor Haile Selassie had been) on ending the long-running guerrilla war in Eritrea and developing its backward economy, whereas the Soviets and Cubans were reluctant to move against Marxists (in Eritrea) hitherto recognized as authentic. Moreover, in Ethiopia as in Angola, they demanded payment for military support and refused to give Ethiopia the kind of economic and technical assistance that it sorely wanted and had hitherto been receiving in generous degree from the West. In the second half of the 1970s, for instance, Marxist Ethiopia received at least fourteen times as much aid from the West as from the Soviet Union. Mozambique was refused admission to Comecon.

In aggregate terms, in the second quinquennium of the 1970s, the Soviet Union extended $335 million in credits, whereas the West, OPEC, and multilateral agencies were sending $57 billion to Africa. Calculated in a more restrictive manner, the flow from the West was still about $35 billion. Taking individual cases in addition to Ethiopia, the comparisons are equally invidious for the Soviet Union.[3] Even the tiny Seychelles, which uniquely has received its arms free, has always gained much more from the West and multilateral agencies than from the Soviets.

In the technical sphere, in the late 1970s the Soviets sent Angola nearly 3,000 Soviet and Eastern European personnel; Nigeria received 1,700, Ethiopia 1,500, Mozambique 800, Guinée 645, and Mali 485. There were between 5,000 and 10,000 noncombatant Cubans in Angola, and fewer than 1,000 in Ethiopia, Guinée, and Mozambique.

Trade with the Soviet Union accounted for no more than 1 percent of imports and exports to and from black Africa. About 75 percent of Africa's trade, both imports and exports, was with the West. For a few countries (Ghana, Guinée, Somalia, Cameroon, and Guinea-Bissau), trade with the Soviet Union was more significant for a few years in the 1960s and 1970s; but even in those countries it was hardly decisive and of only temporary importance. Another significant indicator of African dependence and independence is that only four of the nineteen governments that accepted Soviet arms relied exclusively on the Soviets for equipment. In the 1970s eleven nations received arms primarily from the Soviet Union, but eight also obtained arms from the West.[4]

In the 1980s, African nations discovered again that a heavy dependence upon the Soviet Union was a mixed blessing where it was a blessing at all. Hit hard by the effects of the world recession, by recurrent drought, by persistently poor prices for agricultural and mineral exports, by high costs of imported energy, and by staggering debts, countries friendly to the Soviet Union looked in vain for the kind of investments, purchases, concessions, credits, or grants that would improve their own terms of trade. Instead, everywhere the Soviets remained tightfisted. Moreover, they, too, demanded the repayment of debts. They supported military ventures but almost invariably exacted payments in kind or in foreign exchange. The Angolans and the Ethiopians complained with growing asperity that the Soviets took unfair financial advantage, increasingly found new ways in which to twist the economic screw, and appeared to be unrelenting in their pressure to extend rather than diminish the dependence of their fundamentally weak clients. While the Soviets pressed unremittingly for the establishment of truly vanguard Marxist parties, they also, as in Ethiopia, even compelled their clients to pay the Soviet Union for the costs of shipping heavy equipment back to Moscow for repairs.[5] Even the most entrenched of the Marxist-Leninist states grew to appreciate how disadvantaged they were becoming. Friendship treaties and massive arms transfers brought little economic growth, some but not universal military success, and the erosion of sovereignty. The Soviets often meddled, too, in internal politics and favored cliques within ruling parties and juntas.

The Soviet Union had its own agenda, which rarely respected the nationalist or personalist agendas of Africans. Thus, particularly during a period of Soviet decline, restoring or strengthening ties to the West was seen to have significant merit. Nevertheless, in 1984 Ethiopia inaugurated a new national Communist party, with Mengistu as its leader.

Elsewhere in Africa, southern Africa aside, in 1984 there appeared what can only be described impressionistically as a profound and growing disenchantment with what the Soviet Union had to offer. In Madagascar, Mauritius, and even the Seychelles, there was a perceptible scaling down of pro-Soviet rhetoric and a search for different ways of improving relations with the West. The U.S. invasion of Grenada, interestingly enough, frightened the Seychelles and may have hastened a tendency toward rapprochement and true nonalignment. The Francophone military governments that were Marxist-Leninist or pro-Soviet (Congo, Mali, Benin, Upper Volta) became essentially detached from any deep dependence upon Moscow. Lt. Jerry Rawlings talked about the Soviets in Ghana, but his government was so deeply mired in the slough of profound economic malaise that opportunities for Soviet clientelism were diminished. The big target for the Soviets—Nigeria, with its comparative wealth and burgeoning population (one-quarter of all of Africa)—since the coup at the very end of 1983 slipped farther than ever before from the Soviet grasp.

Given the questionable nature of Soviet penetration of and influence in so much of black Africa, it is on the results of Soviet opportunism in southern Africa that any assessment of the future acceptability and utility of the Soviets must rest. There the Soviet Union confronts the West most strikingly and with potentially great consequences. This is neither a new nor a particularly unusual challenge. But for all its longevity—extending historically into the 1920s—and its widespread acceptability to Africans across a broad front, Soviet policy is and always has been ambiguous, contradictory, and more reactive than assertive. The Soviet Union has benefited from, even depended upon, colonial and Western errors of strategy and tactic, and Western (primarily United States) caution (especially a reluctance to be adventuresome in recognizing and supporting agents of change); but it has rarely sought to explore bold political initiatives or to alter the region's own intrinsic liberationist rhythm or momentum.[6]

In southern Africa the Soviet Union has always fed and continues to feed on the swelling yeast of apartheid. Long ties to the African National Congress (ANC) of South Africa and more recent but equally strong ties to SWAPO of Namibia, the Front for the Liberation of Mozambique (FRELIMO), and the Movement for the Popular Liberation of Angola (MPLA) demonstrate the Soviet Union's willingness to fund and advise the recognized, legitimated, black political and military movements in the richest and most geostrategically important part of the continent. The ANC and SWAPO are liberation movements with insurgent armies in the field, and FRELIMO and the MPLA rule their countries—the MPLA with substantial Soviet support from 1975 to the present.

In the Zimbabwean struggle for independence, the Soviets backed Nkomo's ZAPU, supplied arms, trained top-ranking military officers, provided funds generously during the period of the struggle and after independence, and saw their candidate and their party fail dramatically. The Soviets, like the South Africans (who also backed Nkomo), relied upon a flawed appreciation of Zimbabwean political reality. They must also have gambled upon the enduring appeal of the ideological tenets that accompanied the flow of cash and arms. They ignored—as for racist reasons they do everywhere—evidence of independence among the masses, military cadres, and—most of all—voters. True, the Soviets may have assumed that the British were intent upon rigging the 1980 election in Zimbabwe in favor of Nkomo and that the Soviets were bound to benefit. Or they may have relied cynically upon the likely success of South African intervention on behalf of Nkomo. Nkomo, however, the man for all seasons, was neither capable nor ethnically popular in the postcolonial context. Mugabe and ZANU were much closer to China, Rumania, Yugoslavia, and the nonaligned nations. The Soviet Union, East Germany, and Cuba largely shunned Mugabe's appeal for arms and finance at crucial moments during the run up to settlement and independence. Socialist ties were demonstrably less relevant than clientage and, in this particular case, the globalist struggles between China and the Soviet Union. When Mugabe led ZANU to a largely predictable national triumph and became prime minister, what could have been a centerpiece of Soviet strategy in southern Africa became, instead, one more lost opportunity. Zimbabwe remains suspicious of, if not distinctly hostile to, the Soviet Union. Therefore, despite Zimbabwe's great fear of and antagonism to the West, its failure in Zimbabwe means that the Soviet Union cannot in mid-decade pretend to be in the vanguard of change in the whole region or even uniformly accepted as a welcome patron of that change.

The Soviet Union has established an embassy in Zimbabwe. It has large embassies and listening posts in Botswana and Zambia. But these three sizable presences are useful for the gathering of intelligence much more than for the dissemination of propaganda and the fomenting of local subversion. A few years ago such a generalization could not have been made so confidently; then the Soviets were much more active and successful, particularly in Zambia. In the mid-1980s, however, local experience and impatience with the Soviets, the growing relative strength in the region of South Africa, the passage of time, and changing domestic perspectives have all limited the effective influence of the Soviet Union in these countries. The Soviets also have never had an official presence in Swaziland or Lesotho. Against Lesotho they paradoxically back the Lesotho Liberation Army (LLA), a guerrilla group led by an old-fashioned Marxist, which operates primarily because of South African support.

In southern Africa—outside the theater of operations of South Africa–Namibia and the battleground of Angola, but within the officially Marxist-Leninist states of Angola and Mozambique—the Soviet Union in the mid-1980s has lost its forward role and any pretension to serious leadership. So long as South Africa continues powerful and white-ruled, however, and so long as grand apartheid denies political participation to the majority of the people of South Africa, the Soviet Union will retain a moral advantage and an inevitable political presence in the eyes and minds of the governing groups of the black nation-states of the region. Indeed, the states that now maintain their distance from the Soviets and are less than anxious to receive Cuban or East German proxy technicians and advisers are nevertheless conscious of the utility of a Soviet counterforce. The Soviets remain a support of last resort. No matter how vaguely or even inaccurately, the black states that have wrenched themselves away from the Soviet orbit still depend upon the possibility of Soviet military intervention to keep South African adventurism in check. At least, that is a theoretical and untested assumption. Certainly, constructive engagement has proved no ultimate shield for the black states of southern Africa against South African hegemonic drives. In the later 1980s, no matter the fundamental wish of the black states to rely and depend upon Western and U.S. protection, they cannot and should not.

The striking central variable in the southern African equation is the enormous growth since 1980 of South African power relative to the West, relative to the liberation movements (although the ANC is more potent than it was), and relative to the Soviet Union and its proxies. The South African military establishment in 1983 included a standing army of 83,000 men (about 5 or 6 percent black), a conscript force bringing the army's total strength to 250,000, a navy and an air force of 5,000 and 10,000 respectively, and a total mobilizable potential—based on commandos or reserves—of about 400,000.[7] Of great importance is the South African military machine's overall self-sufficiency. The state-owned Armscor supplies jet fighters and small arms, howitzers, and grenades, and machine guns and signal equipment. South African avionics is weak and dependent on outside suppliers. Otherwise the military might of the country draws upon self-sufficient resources. Admittedly, South Africa has no indigenous petroleum, but this deficit has been largely eliminated by stockpiling and by oil from coal facilities which now supply about 50 percent of all of South Africa's petroleum needs.[8]

To a striking degree, South Africa has already demonstrated its military capacities and capabilities. From 1978, but more decisively from 1981 to 1984, South Africa extended its military frontier beyond Namibia deeply into southern Angola. Without serious challenge by SWAPO, the MPLA army, the 30,000 Cubans in Angola, or the 3,000 East German or Soviet advisers there, South Africa maintained control of the skies, destroyed installations on the ground, and audaciously even moved in troops to establish a commanding presence on the territory of a state distant from its own borders. At the same time, South Africa strengthened its military grip in Namibia; 25,000 South African troops were based along its northern marches through 1984. Furthermore, a large (20,000-man) South African—backed and —supplied insurgent group, the Union for the Total Independence of Angola (UNITA), has operated with more and more impunity from southern Angola against the MPLA. Indeed, in recent years UNITA, closely cooperating with South Africa, has been able to strike decisively against the MPLA in the purlieu of Angola's capital and well across the central rail line into the diamondiferous lands of northeastern Angola. Even with Soviet backing and Cuban soldiers, the MPLA government has been wholly unable to oust or even to curb the power and spread of the UNITA insurgency.

As South Africa has since 1980 thoroughly destabilized Angola; checked if not overwhelmed the SWAPO guerrillas based since 1977 in Angola (earlier they were in Zambia); and weakened the MPLA government to the point that it is credibly contemplating changing its international allegiances and considering a coalition with UNITA, its arch enemy, so South Africa since 1980 has cowed little Lesotho and manipulated Swaziland, compelling both weak states to bar their borders to the ANC and end the flow of saboteurs across the hills and plains of rural South Africa toward its white-inhabited industrial heartland. So, too, since 1980 has South Africa developed, funded, and armed the Mozambique National Resistance Movement (MNR). By backing the LLA, UNITA, and the MNR, South Africa had added to its own impressive military punch and its suzerainty in the region. Ineffectively countered, if at all, by the diplomacy of constructive engagement, this multiarmored South African juggernaut emerged by the mid-1980s as an instrument of profound and decisive regional policy relevance.

South Africa has the only durable economy in the region, or even in much of Africa. Based on the export of gold and other minerals, with an effective manufacturing capacity and a healthy agricultural sector, South Africa—however weakened or crippled temporarily by recession and, even more, a refusal to share its overall wealth with Africans—is strong compared to its historically poorer neighbors. Only Zimbabwe and Angola have economies that could be and have been robust regionally, but the first has been undermined by drought and mistimed official rhetoric and the second hit hard by war. Mozambique, even more vulnerable because of its weak base, its attention to ideology rather than incentive-based growth, drought, and the cyclone of 1984, was finally pushed to its economic knees by the MNR insurgency. Angola, bled by the campaign against UNITA and the consequent need to pay in kind for Soviet and Cuban help by limiting growth and subsidizing the export to the eastern bloc and Cuba of oil, coffee, diamonds, and iron ore, has also been compelled by South African–arranged circumstances to put economic reality before political objective. A recent account estimated that the Angolan government was paying between $14,000 and $22,000 a year for each Soviet and Cuban soldier, amounts contributing to a total daily cost of the war against South Africa and its proxies of about $4 million. (To the resentment of Angolans, these payments to the Soviets and Cubans apparently bought little friendship: the Soviets and Cubans sunbathed on separate, guarded, segregated beaches and shopped in special foreign-currency stores.)[9]

In Angola and Mozambique, the Marxist-Leninist governments have found ideology and east bloc support no shelter against South African–inspired storms and other calamities. They have had to sue for peace and, by so doing, to cripple if not end Soviet claims to paramountcy in much if not all of the southern African region. Potentially, the events now unfolding in Angola, Mozambique, Namibia, and South Africa will strengthen South African power for the rest of the 1980s and move the region well away from the Soviet orbit.

Both the Mozambiquan and Angolan *volte faces* have been effected under duress. Nonetheless, Mozambique, conscious both of its inherent fragility and of the Soviet Union's inability—and unwillingness—to provide the economic and military might with which to counter South Africa, decided early in 1984 to trade its fraternal alliance with the ANC for support from South Africa. The government of Mozambique did not break with the Soviet Union, renounce its friendship treaty, or offer to alter its internal economic system. It did, however, oust the individual Soviet-aligned leaders of the ANC military wing and faithfully promise to prevent ANC attacks upon South Africa from Mozambiquan territory. "My country will not serve as a base for attacks or violence against the territory of South Africa," said General Jacínto Soares Veloso, Mozambique's minister of economic affairs, in the presence of the South African foreign minister.[10] The agreement angered the ANC as well as the Kremlin; but Mozambique had, its leaders said, been compelled to choose South African tourism and trade, and the promised end of destabilization against Mozambique, over continuing to work with the ANC and the Soviet Union. If Mozambique continues to move demonstrably from near Soviet clientage to an Afro-socialist economic orientation and dependence upon friendship and cooperation with the West and South Africa, then the reputation of the Soviet Union in Africa will have fallen further.

Angola assented to a cease-fire in 1984, and South Africa agreed to withdraw from Angolan territory. Angola has promised to prevent SWAPO guerrillas from moving back into the Angolan territory vacated by the South Africans or from crossing from Angola into Namibia. By this accord, however, South Africa was not prevented from continuing to back UNITA with arms, diesel fuel, and funds. Nor was the final disposition mentioned of the South African–backed mercenary battalions that have been attached to UNITA. South African air reconnaissance of southern Angola was not curtailed by any agreement. Furthermore, Angola and South Africa (with some U.S. presence) in 1984 established a joint monitoring group to police the cease-fire. All of these changes were accomplished despite the existence in Angola of a strong Soviet military and security influence and of numerous Cubans. The cease-fire was an acknowledgment of the diplomatic facilitating efforts of the United States and the presumed visible weakness in the region of the Soviet Union.

The Soviet Union could not oust South Africa from Angola, although a diplomatic démarche by the Soviets in late 1983 helped to concentrate the South African official mind. The Soviets either could not protect the MPLA or were perceived by the MPLA to be unreliable. Likewise the Cubans. The MPLA, weakened by South Africa and UNITA, economically starved by the Soviets and their own mismanagement, and persuaded that recognition by the United States would mean economic assistance, became prepared in 1985 to diminish its reliance on the Soviet Union and chance some kind of merger with or absorption by UNITA. This was such a risky strategy that its obverse, profound Soviet weakness, is demonstrative. Moreover, if weakness it is, it is a weakness by choice. "Southern Africa," writes Legvold, "is not likely to be the place where the Soviet Union settles scores with the Reagan administration or chooses to face down the United States." Yet he anticipates a more aggressive Soviet posture and active antagonism to South Africa.[11] The Soviet Union could turn nasty in the region (although it is hardly an autonomous agent), but at mid-decade the Angolans have apparently decided that a reliance upon Soviet firepower will prove less productive for them than accommodating South Africa's might.

The United States wants these sharp reversals in Soviet credibility to pave the way for the long-deferred settlement of the problem of Namibia. If the MPLA ultimately allows the proverbial UNITA camel to stick its nose under the government's tent, if the Soviet Union does not attempt to replace today's Angolan junta with one more intransigent, and if the Cubans do begin to go home, then the Soviet backing for SWAPO becomes as inconsequential as observers have always predicted, and South Africa will easily be able to risk an internationally sponsored election that would anoint SWAPO as independent Namibia's ruling party.[12] Namibia could then proceed to independence in accord with the provisions of Security Council Resolution 435. Thus, according to a scenario for Namibia that would build upon South Africa's trumping of Soviet ambitions in the region, a Marxist-backed party could come to power in Namibia without arousing many South African fears, and therefore with South African acquiescence. The Marxist nature of SWAPO, however, would be of more historical than contemporary relevance, for the center of gravity in the region would by then have moved even more decisively from Moscow and Havana to Pretoria.

Either way, South Africa wins and the Soviet Union loses. Although the West wants South Africa to modernize apartheid and move toward fuller participatory government for all its citizens, the weaker the Soviet Union becomes regionally, the less urgent will be the West's motivations. Indeed, this is precisely what South Africa has in mind. It wants to use its flexed strength to gain a freedom from external interference. Whether it chooses to use such a newly achieved freedom to evolve politically, as constructive engagement assumes, or whether it merely chooses to make a few tactical adjustments, is a question for the future.

The South African contest has been less against the Soviet Union, despite lip service paid to the concept of countering the "total onslaught" by a "total strategy," than it has been a battle against the African National Congress.[13] Organized in 1912 as the premier African political organization in a country where Africans had almost no political rights, the ANC operated until the late 1940s and early 1950s as a reformist body, largely representative of the black elite.[14] Then, with the coming of rigid apartheid after the revolutionary victory of the Nationalist party in 1948 and the consolidation of its power in 1951 and 1956, the ANC become more strident in its protest. Boycotts and demonstrations were followed by protomilitancy. By the mid-1950s the ANC was working closely with supporters of the South African Communist party (which had been banned in 1950); by 1960, itself banned, the ANC went both underground (a tactic that failed) and into exile.

Only since 1977, backed by the Soviet Union and bolstered by young recruits from Soweto, has the ANC become a credible guerrilla threat to

South Africa. Incidents have increased by a hundredfold in five years; and their seriousness and severity (the Pretoria bombing of 1983, the sabotage of the Koeberg nuclear reactor and the Sasol oil-from-coal plant, and so on) was not minimized by the South African security forces. Trial after trial of ANC guerrillas showed how cells had penetrated South Africa and how much the state worried about insurgency. Nevertheless, in 1985 ANC military cadres numbered no more than 2,500; the Soviet Union had not armed the ANC dramatically. Nor was it clear from the tactics of the ANC that the Soviet Union either believed that South Africa was ripe for revolution or was persuaded that the ANC could or should be the revolution's chosen instrument.[15]

If South Africa can convert its present tactical advantage into a strategic commitment, then the influence of the Soviet Union will continue to be immeasurably weakened in the region. Despite the persistence, unchecked, of apartheid, the economic and political fragility of the Soviet clients will have limited the ability of Soviet policies to prevail regionally. There is still time for the Soviet Union to mount a counterattack—but with what ammunition? Over the years, in this region and elsewhere in Africa, it has forfeited its influence by a set of miserly assistance policies and, it seems, by its awareness of the limits of Soviet interest and hence power in such distant regions. Because the Soviet Union has pursued its policies very much on the cheap, and—from the African point of view—not only parsimoniously but pusillanimously, it has fostered the cynicism rather than the loyalty of Africans. Their indoctrination has been shallow, and their commitment to anything other than opportunism has been more and more limited by the ineffectuality of Soviet action. Again, this consequence rebounds to the benefit of the West but is a result of a not improper assessment of the real interests of the Soviet Union much more than of successful Western countertactics. Even given the perpetuation of apartheid and the West's inextricable association with South Africa (past, present, and future), the Soviet Union has, in African eyes, been restrained and insufficiently active, as befits its ultimate self-interest.

Are these trends, profoundly disappointing as they must be to the Soviets, reversible? Given Africa's broad exposure to Soviet stinginess, timorousness, churlishness, and recent failure, it is hard in the mid-1980s to predict a Soviet recovery. Africans must acknowledge Soviet assistance in Angola, Ethiopia and elsewhere, but they now know the deeper costs of that assistance. They also discern the limits of Soviet interest and power, especially in the unremitting confrontation between Africa and South Africa. Conscious of South African strength and Soviet weakness, aware of a dependence upon the West for intercession and mediation, and everywhere reminded of their own intrinsic fragility, the major and many minor players of African power politics are refusing to barter their sovereignty to the Soviets for what are increasingly seen as ephemeral gains. Only when and if Soviet military might delivers SWAPO or the ANC to power in Namibia and South Africa will Africa look anew in the Soviet direction.

Notes

1. David E. Albright, *The USSR and Sub-Saharan Africa in the 1980's* (New York, 1983).
2. Robert Legvold, "The Soviet Threat to Southern Africa," chapter 3 of this book, 36.
3. Albright, *The USSR and Sub-Saharan Africa,* 27–28.
4. Albright, *The USSR and Sub-Saharan Africa,* 29–31. See also Seth Singleton, "The Shared Tactical Goals of South Africa and the Soviet Union," *CSIS Africa Notes, 12* (26 April 1983), 2.
5. *Washington Post,* 25 January 1984; *Boston Globe,* 8 March 1984.
6. Legvold, "Soviet Threat," 39.
7. But see Pauline Baker, "South Africa's Strategic Vulnerabilities: The Citadel Assumption Reconsidered," *African Studies Review, 20* (1977), 89–99.
8. For details see Robert I. Rotberg, *Suffer the Future: Policy Choices in Southern Africa* (Cambridge, Mass., 1980), 120–122.
9. *Christian Science Monitor,* 20 January 1984; Singleton "Tactical Goals," 1.
10. *The New York Times,* 3 March 1984.
11. Legvold, "Soviet Threat," 49.
12. See Robert I. Rotberg, "Political and Economic Realities in a Time of Settlement," in idem. (ed.), *Namibia: Political and Economic Prospects* (Lexington, Mass., 1983), 37–38.
13. For the notion of total onslaught, see Robert I. Rotberg, above, 17.
14. See Gail M. Gerhart, *Black Power in South Africa: The Evolution of an Ideology* (Berkeley, 1978), 21–44; Rotberg, *Suffer,* 62.
15. For a cogent analysis, see Legvold, "Soviet Threat," 43–44.

5
Economic Interests and Security Issues in Southern Africa

Henry S. Bienen

Southern Africa: Economic Background

South Africa is able to wield a large economic stick vis-à-vis its neighbors in southern Africa. It can provide important carrots to those neighbors and to African countries farther north through technical assistance, aid, and trade relations. The relative strength of South Africa's economy among weak African ones is evident.

South Africa is a major economic power in Africa and in southern Africa. This point is clear from the comparative statistics on income levels and rates of growth (see table 5–1 for southern African comparisons). South Africa is the only African country other than the oil exporters, Libya and Algeria, ranked by the World Bank as upper-middle-income. South Africa's annual rate of gross national product (GNP) growth per capita between 1960 and 1981 was 2.3 percent. This is low for the period compared to the rate for industrial countries and for upper-middle-income developing countries such as Malaysia, Mexico, Brazil, and Korea. Given the poor performances of African economies in the 1970s, however, few (Kenya, Lesotho, Cameroon, Tunisia, Malawi, Egypt, Nigeria) have growth rates above South Africa's and only a few (Togo and Ivory Coast) have rates close to South Africa's.[1]

The *World Development Report* does not provide information about the sectoral rates of growth of South Africa's economy. Data on the structure of the economy make it clear that only Zimbabwe among black African countries comes close to South Africa in terms of industrialization and the share of product occupied by the manufacturing sector.[2] South Africa does not have a really buoyant performance for food production. Its average index of food production per capita for 1979–1981 is 104 against a base of 1969–1971. However, only Ivory Coast and Tunisia do better in Africa during this period.[3] Only South Africa has been a reliable exporter of food grains in Africa during the 1970s—

Table 5–1
Southern African Economies

Country	Area (000 km²)	Population, mid-1981	GNP Per Capita, 1981	GNP Average Annual Growth (%), 1980–1981	GDP, Millions of Dollars	Average Annual Growth Rate (%), Gross Domestic Investment 1970–1981
Angola	1,247	7.8	470[a]	-2.3[a]	2,580	-9.0[a]
Botswana[a]	600	0.8	910	9.2		2.8
Lesotho	30	1.4	540	4.1	320	19.3
Malawi	118	6.2	200	2.7	1,420	2.8
Mozambique	802	12.5	230[a]	-0.1[a]	2,360	-8.4[a]
South Africa	1,221	29.5	2,770	2.3	6,980	3.2
Swaziland[a]	17	0.6	680	6.2		
Tanzania	945	19.1	280	-0.2	4,350	3.7
Zaire	2,354	29.8	210	-0.1	5,380	7.3
Zambia	753	5.8	600	0.0	3,430	-10.8
Zimbabwe	391	7.2	870	1.0	6,010	

Source: 1983 *World Development Report* tables.

[a]All figures for Botswana and Swaziland are from the 1982 *World Development Report* and are for mid-1980.
All figures except areas and populations for Mozambique are from the 1982 *World Development Report*.
Some figures for Angola are from the 1982 *World Development Report*.

1980s, failing to export only in years of disastrous drought such as 1982–1983.

The magnitude of South Africa's development compared to that of other African countries can best be seen by looking at comparative per capita energy-consumption figures. South Africa's is four to six times larger than those of most North African countries and eight to fifteen times larger than those of most black African countries. South Africa does do better than other African countries on quality-of-life indicators—indicators such as life expectancy and daily per capita calorie supply—but not so much better as its higher income and development levels would imply.[4] On the other hand, in terms of technological and infrastructural development, comparisons show a South African position in Africa that is at least as high as predictions from per capita energy consumption. South Africa has technologies in mining and in coal-to-liquid fuel and nuclear energy that are advanced by world standards. It has its own armaments production industries. Its equipment superiority (not to say its ability to maintain equipment and keep advanced arms in the field) is great.[5]

Patterns of Dependence

South Africa exports more to African states than it imports. Although trade between South Africa and individual states is not broken down publicly, South African exports to Africa more than doubled between 1970 and 1980. Food, manufactured goods, and petroleum products account for important shares of South Africa's exports to southern African states. These states are heavily dependent on South Africa, especially for transport machinery and plastics. South Africa itself buys electricity generated by Mozambique's Cahora Bassa Dam, receiving supplies amounting in the past to some 10 percent of the South African Electricity Supply Commission (ESCOM) total supplies; but it sells electricity to Mozambique, Lesotho, Namibia, Swaziland, and Zimbabwe.[6] Botswana has asked to be linked to the South African power grid.[7]

By 1980, according to the Department of Customs and Excise in Pretoria, South Africa's exports to African countries exceeded $1 billion. Imports rose to a record $345 million for the January–November period in 1980.[8] Most of South Africa's African trade is with southern African states. Tanzania and Angola have the least trade with South Africa among the nine states of the southern African region.[9] South Africa's trade relations with southern Africa are not reciprocal. Whereas over a third of Mozambique's trade and over a quarter of Zimbabwe's is with South Africa, South Africa exports more to Britain or Switzerland than the 10 percent of its exports that go to all of Africa (see table 5–2).[10] On the imports side, South Africa receives only 2 percent from all of Africa. Unofficial trade through middlemen, if counted, would produce some-what higher trade figures for South Africa with Africa than official South African figures, but the share of trade with Africa would remain relatively small.

Trade of southern African countries with South Africa is asymmetrical. What is not crucial for South Africa is crucial for many of its trade partners in southern Africa. For Botswana, Lesotho, and Swaziland, trade with South Africa is overwhelmingly important. For Mozambique it is crucial, and has risen, not fallen, in the last few years. Zimbabwe's trade with South Africa has fallen as a share of its total trade since independence, but it has not fallen in absolute terms; 40 percent of its manufacturing exports went to South Africa on preferential terms until South Africa temporarily annulled a seventeen-year-old trade-preference agreement in 1981.[11] Zambia has been able to diversify trade away from South Africa; Angola and Tanzania have never been large trade partners of South Africa. For Malawi, trade with South Africa is important, and South Africa provides some key exports to Zaire.

Although we should not exaggerate the tightness and comprehensiveness of southern Africa as an economic region, this area constitutes a regional economic subsystem more than any other part of Africa because trade relations are relatively extensive and because transport and communications facilities link the region. Also, labor migrates from southern African states to South Africa. Formal agreements link Bot-

Table 5–2
Selected South African Export Markets
In US $ million

	1970	1973	1976	1979
United Kingdom	624	1,010	1,147	1,121
United States	181	232	527	1,908
Argentina	3	4	9	190
Brazil	1	11	31	120
Taiwan	1	25	172	246
Israel	5	24	36	125
Venezuela	4	12	69	20
Africa	369	446	521	617

Source: IMF, *Direction of Trade Yearbook,* 1975 and 1980 (Washington, D.C.: IMF). Data from *South African Digest,* August 29, 1980, p. 2. As found in Timothy M. Shaw, "South Africa, Southern Africa, and the World System," in Thomas M. Callaghy, (ed.,) *South Africa in Southern Africa* (New York, 1983), Table 3.1, p. 55.

swana, Swaziland, and Lesotho through the Southern Africa Customs Union (SACU) and Lesotho and Swaziland through the Rand Monetary Area (RMA), to which Namibia also belongs.

At present, a network of transport and communication grids, labor migration patterns, and formal economic unions lead to a pattern of dependence of southern African states on South Africa. The dependence is not now a mutual one (see figure 5–1). Copper and other mineral exports from Zaire, Zimbabwe, and Zambia must exit through South Africa and Mozambique's ports or take a longer and more costly rail and road path through to Tanzania's clogged ports via uncertain transport systems. The Angolan civil war has led to the closing of the Benguela railway, making that route only marginally usable. Only Mozambique can easily ship its goods through its own ports; but Mozambique, too, earns revenue from the shipment of South African exports through its harbors. Mozambique uses South African technicians to manage its own ports. Moreover, alternative shipping and transport facilities through Mozambique are highly vulnerable to sabotage, as they have been since 1981 due to the depredations of the South African-backed MNR insurgent movement.[12] South Africa can also prevent or slow up the railway stock, maintenance equipment, and technical assistance to keep Zimbabwe's railways moving. It brought chaos to Zimbabwe in 1982 by delaying petrol and railway imports, and it produced similar results with a slowdown of imports to Lesotho in June 1983. By its support for UNITA and by its own military reach to Angola, South Africa can keep the Benguela railway cut, preventing copper exports from Zambia and Zaire across Angola.[13]

As in trade, the transport dependencies between South Africa and its neighbors are not mutual. It is true that South Africa's own ports are congested and that it is easier to export from the Transvaal abroad via Mozambique's ports. Thus freight increased on the railways from South Africa to Mozambique from 15,000 to 30,000 tons a day between 1980 and 1981.[14] About 15–17 percent of South Africa's exports go through Mozambique. Indeed, although the MNR has disrupted power grids, the railway continued to operate with difficulty to Mozambique's ports. A disruption of Mozambique's railways would raise costs to South Africa; a disruption of South Africa's railways for Zimbabwe and the BLS states would be extremely serious. Although Zambia can now export through the Tazara railway, this is an uncertain proposition given the state of Tanzania's ports and railway maintenance. For Mozambique itself, freight charges on South African exports are a major foreign-exchange earner.

The movement of labor from southern African states to South Africa

Figure 5–1. Southern African Rail Networks

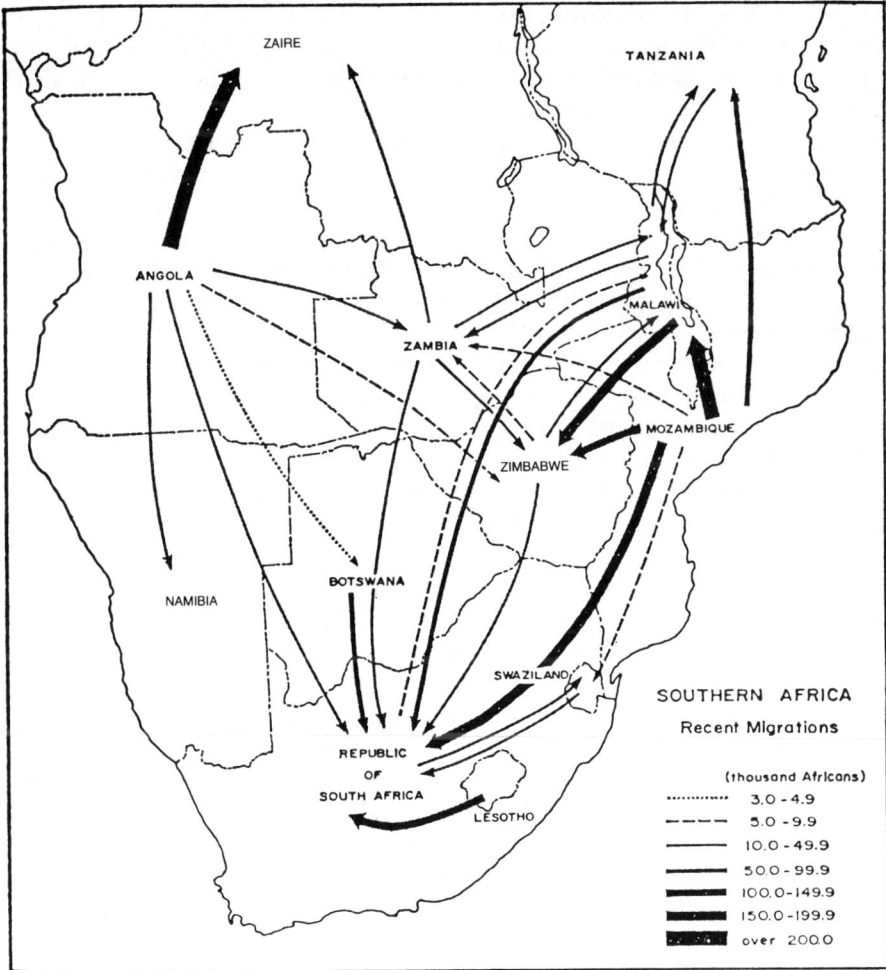

Source: Kenneth W. Grundy, *Confrontation and Accommodation in Southern Africa: The Limits of Independence*, (Berkeley, 1973), 61, used by permission of the University of California Press.

Figure 5–2. Migration of Foreign Africans

is characterized also by asymmetrical relationships (see figure 5–2). South Africa employs migrant labor from all the neighboring states except Zambia. Although the number of foreign workers used as migrant laborers has been reduced over the last years, non–South African workers make up over 40 percent of the total mining work force.[15] South Africa might prefer to use labor from Botswana, Lesotho, and Mozambique for political and economic leverage against those countries; it might also want fewer South African blacks in the mines. But it has reduced the number of migrants. In 1974 a little more than 20 percent of workers in the mines were from South Africa; by 1981 they accounted for 60 percent.[16] The largest decline was from Mozambique. Cuts in migrant workers to South Africa seriously affect the foreign-exchange earnings of southern African states. Malawi, Botswana, and Lesotho all had more migrant laborers abroad than they had wage earners at home, although not all were in South Africa.[17]

Along with trade and control of transport networks, South Africa uses preferences and subsidies as well as technical assistance, aid, and direct investment to further its goals. South Africa ceased to subsidize wheat and maize to Lesotho in 1976.[18] After Zaire left the Central Selling Organization (De Beers Ltd.) for diamonds, it found it more costly to market its own diamonds. South Africa's direct investment in Zimbabwe and Namibia is very large.

Although all the southern African states except Tanzania have some dependence on South Africa, the type and degree of intensity differs between states. For some, the transport and communication grids are in South Africa's hands. This is true for Zimbabwe, Zambia, and the BLS states; to lesser extents for Angola, Zaire, and Malawi; and even for Mozambique. Some are major exporters of labor to South Africa, including the BLS states, Zimbabwe, Mozambique, and Malawi. All but Tanzania, Angola, and Zambia import large quantities from South Africa and significant shares of exports of Zimbabwe, Namibia, and the BLS states go to or through South Africa.

Economics and Security

What is clear, and has been so from the start of South Africa's economic relations with African states, is that economic cooperation and economic punishment are in the service of South Africa's foreign-policy goals and domestic-security concerns. There does not appear in the South African scheme of things to be a so-called low politics of economic policy and economic affairs.[19] Economic policies toward African states are very direct instruments for political influence.[20]

South Africa's attitudes and policies toward economic ties and economic development in southern Africa have been determined by political and security concerns from the time that black African states became independent until the collapse of white power in the Portuguese territories and in Rhodesia. (Zaire, 1960; Tanzania, 1961; Malawi and Zambia, 1964; Botswana and Lesotho, 1966; Swaziland, 1968; Mozambique and Angola, 1975; Zimbabwe, 1980.) At no time have economic factors in themselves governed South Africa's policies. When South Africa has moved to reach out to black African states—first under Prime Minister Verwoerd and then, after 1966, more eagerly under Prime Minister Vorster and Foreign Minister Hilgard Muller—it held out various economic benefits. It maintained some of those benefits even during periods when it was actively punishing neighboring states. Thus, although South Africa recently has made military incursions into Lesotho and Mozambique, it did not cut off all economic ties with these countries. It has, however, used its economic relations as a weapon first and foremost.

South Africa sustained the Smith rebellion in Rhodesia at some economic cost, and it ended its support not when the economic pinch became too great but when it decided that for security and political purposes a continuation of a white regime in Rhodesia was more of a problem than an advantage. South Africa seems willing to sustain its positions in Namibia despite significant financial costs. It is hard to see that its Namibian policies, any more than the policies that evolved towards Rhodesia-Zimbabwe, are governed primarily by a calculation of economic costs and benefits or by any long-run economic advantages to maintaining the positions of white minority regimes. Rather, these policies, like earlier ones, have been determined more by external security concerns and internal domestic political ones.

This is not to imply that South Africa has never had economic interests in mind when formulating its policies toward states to the north. South Africa moved into mining, fishing, and manufacturing projects in the Portuguese colonies. It invested heavily in both the Cahora Bassa dam on the Zambezi above Tete and in the Kunene dam in southern Angola, near the Namibian border.[21] South Africa was interested in buying large amounts of the projected power of these dams and in using water for irrigation. South Africa's access to hydroelectric power, however, has not depended on good relations with Angola and Mozambique, and it has been certainly willing to put at risk those relations. Indeed, it has supported the MNR in Mozambique, which blew up facilities that cost South Africa access to Cahora Bassa's electricity source. Whether or not the MNR was given a green light, the South Africans know that insurgent movements cannot be controlled closely and that insurrection and warfare in Angola and Mozambique put infrastructure in jeopardy, including facilities that South Africa itself values. Because of the Angolan war, the hydroelectric station on the Kunene at the Ruacana Falls at first was used only occasionally.[22]

There has been frequent discussion of economic regionalism in southern Africa and of building political ties on the basis of economic cooperation. The prospects for economic cooperation during times when South Africa was reaching out to neighboring states, and when a number of those states were not yet independent, was predicated on friendly foreign relations. At the core of economic cooperation from South Africa's point of view, however, was a demand that the establishment by South Africa of separate states for its so-called Bantu populations (the homelands) be accepted.[23] The idea of friendly foreign relations was easier to postulate when Angola, Mozambique, and Rhodesia were ruled by whites and when Malawi seemed to accept South Africa's provisos in the late 1960s and early 1970s.[24] The collapse of Portuguese rule in the mid-1970s altered prospects irrevocably for what South Africa called a possible Commonwealth of Southern Africa. The independence of Zimbabwe was simply the nail in the coffin of this idea.

Southern African states have maintained economic relations with South Africa out of dependence and necessity, but they would not agree to accept the homelands policy and to acquiesce in the system of separate development. They would only cease to give aid and succor to South African dissidents under military and economic pressures. These the South Africans applied extensively in what has come to be called the policy of destabilization.

Short of intense economic and military pressure, South Africa was not able to translate its economic power into political influence in southern Africa in the 1970s. It could not prohibit independence for Angola, Mozambique, and Zimbabwe. It could not make those states friendly to it after they became independent. It could be argued that South Africa lost regional power throughout the 1970s even though the black African states' economic performances were not strong and South Africa remained as economically dominant as it had been. What South Africa has been able to do is to exploit internal divisions in Angola, and it may possibly be able to do so in the future in Zimbabwe. It has supported dissidents in Mozambique and Lesotho, and it has taken advantage of structural weaknesses and economic policy mistakes to increase its economic leverage over Mozambique.

Where economic leverage has been not extensive—in Angola as compared to Mozambique, Zimbabwe, and the BLS states—South Africa's own military involvement and the magnitude of military support for UNITA have been crucial in helping to weaken the MPLA regime. The latter's own weakness and inability to come to political terms with its opponents are relevant, of course. South Africa, however, has not turned its economic strength directly into consistent political leverage over states aside from the BLS ones.[25] For the larger states, and even for Botswana and Lesotho at various times, South Africa has not faced completely compliant states. It has made the southern African states lessen their support for insurgents through economic strangulation, or the threat of it, and through direct military punishment. Economic carrots, however, have not allowed South Africa to have its way, nor has economic pressure, unless carried far, been completely effective.

South Africa can get its way in the short and medium runs by using strong economic and military pressure. But it will not be able to create security for itself or get acceptance of its internal policies via what has, at various times, been called a "coprosperity sphere" or a "southern African commonwealth of states," or most recently a "constellation of states."[26] The last would involve monetary arrangements such as those of the Rand Monetary Union, a southern African multilateral development bank, customs unions, industrialization location cooperation, and regional development cooperation. Although there may be advantages to neighboring states in the formation of regional organizations for economic development, political considerations that revolve around South Africa's domestic policies will preclude states from cooperative ventures beyond what economic necessity requires.

It is true that political power is often highly centralized in black African states, especially in the spheres of foreign policy and foreign economic policy. Domestic interest groups which might put pressure on foreign affairs are weak. Foreign-policy bureaucracies that might constrain leaders' prerogatives are undeveloped. Nonetheless, South Africa's policies constitute an issue that in many black African states unifies rathei than splits elites, and also engages the attention of masses of Africans. Thus any overt southern African compliance with South Africa, beyond what is deemed necessary, would be extremely difficult for most states. Of course, elites may make their own private deals and transactions, as they have done in Zaire, Malawi, and even Kenya. Few states, however, have adopted Malawi's relatively open economic stance toward South Africa, and no others have established diplomatic relations with it.[27] Even Malawi has at various times cut back on sending labor migrants to South Africa (only to reverse itself and resume labor migration in 1977) and has tried to avoid South Africa's complete embrace. Malawi has also joined the Southern African Development Coordinating Conference (SADCC).

SADCC and Regional Cooperation

It is not just political aversion to South Africa's racial and constitutional policies that makes states leery of economic arrangements with that country. Nor is it only that southern African states fear that a "constel-

lation of states" would encourage and legitimate South Africa's homelands policies, linking the homelands to the BLS and other states in parallel
arrangements. It is also that small states fear the economic embrace of a
larger, more powerful neighbor.[28] Even if South Africa were to be ruled
by blacks, we can conjecture that southern African states would show a
degree of ambivalence similar to that which has marked West African
states' attitudes toward Nigeria and that country's dominant role in the
Economic Community of West African States (ECOWAS). Nigeria has
trodden lightly for the most part, given the economic and political sen-
sitivities of its ECOWAS partners, but it also used its oil as a weapon
against Ghana after the first Rawlings coup. It has rapidly and brutally
repatriated hundreds of thousands of Ghanaians, Chadians, and people
from Niger and Cameroon. Its markets are an attraction, as are its resources, but its size and weight also make other states nervous.

South Africa's economy is in many ways even more dominant vis-à-
vis its neighbors than is Nigeria's compared to other West African states.
South Africa's transport grid gives greater leverage, as does its technological advancement; it has more effective military might compared to
its neighbors than Nigeria has compared to states in West Africa. Thus,
politics apart, southern African states might look for cooperative arrangements, but they would also look for ways to lessen their dependence on South Africa and would be fearful of its power. They fear that
formal economic arrangements would build in and institutionalize South
Africa's central position.[29] Politics are not apart, of course, and South
Africa has used its economic power in a coercive fashion.

Thus, despite the southern African states' argument that SADCC is
not directed against South Africa, SADCC clearly is an attempt to lessen
dependence on South Africa and to create economic alternatives to the
South African giant.[30] Indeed, in policy terms, SADCC has come to be
a mirror of South Africa's own linkage of regional economic cooperation
and domestic politics. South Africa has in mind tighter integration with
and greater dependence of southern African economies on its own economy. The SADCC countries want to reduce South African leverage by
linking the southern African states with new rail and road networks
estimated to cost at least $2 billion over a decade.[31] Moreover, South
Africa has hoped that a constellation of states would allow it to proceed
with its homelands policy. SADCC countries, as well as the donors who
will bear the burdens of SADCC's transport, communications, agricultural, and health investments, hope that economic development in southern Africa will improve political stability, thus showing South Africa that
neighboring African states can both develop and rule themselves without
strife. It is argued that if they can, then South Africans at least will
reassess their views on sharing power among its peoples. Also, it has

been suggested that a major donor commitment to SADCC will show South Africa that Western countries are serious about aligning them-selves with forces of change in South Africa.[32] Another presumed benefit from helping southern African states to develop would be a lessening of Western dependence on the mineral flows from South Africa. South Africa would control copper exports from Zaire and Zambia less if new transport grids were created. Similarly, chrome exports from Zimbabwe and possibly other mineral exports from that country could, it is argued, be exported through Mozambique's ports, thus lessening South Africa's control of strategic minerals.

Western Interests

The United States and especially Europe have a vested interest in main-taining access to minerals from southern Africa. The creation of new transport grids would lead to a greater possibility for exporting minerals from southern Africa if instability increased within South Africa itself and if that country's own transport and mining facilities were endan-gered. However, if South Africa felt that neighboring countries were supporting insurgents who put its own infrastructure and production at risk, we can only assume that it would lash out at neighboring states as it already has done in Lesotho and Mozambique and extensively in An-gola. Thus the only way to guarantee access to southern Africa's strategic minerals is to create stability within the region as a whole. This means that South Africa must have an internal evolution such that the risks of domestic insurgency are lessened and that neighboring states feel that change is occurring in a positive direction. At the same time, South Africa must believe that its neighbors are willing to allow for positive evolution and not try to destabilize it. For although the means of destabilization on the part of southern African states in South Africa are at present less than South Africa's abilities to disrupt their economies and polities, South Africa is not without long-run security concerns.

Do the Western powers have anything to fear from a southern Af-rican minerals cartel if economic and political cooperation could be con-structed in the region? It is true that a substantial share of the world reserves of gold, manganese, vanadium, platinum, and chromium are located in South Africa (plus Zimbabwe for chromium). A major pro-portion of the world's principal cobalt reserves are in Zaire and Zambia. The Soviet Union is another repository of platinum-based metals, man-ganese, and gold. It cannot be a large market for southern African min-erals, but its cooperation is necessary for price collusion. It has little to offer in the way of economic assistance.

There are major disputes among analysts concerning the probability, duration, and impact of interruptions in mineral supplies. There are also disputes about the impact of new technologies, especially deep-sea mining for manganese, cobalt, copper, and nickel; and there are uncertainties about the likelihood of major new discoveries. Different judgments about Western vulnerabilities rest also on assessments of the potential for conservation, recycling, demand-reducing technologies, and substitution of other minerals.[33] However, there is little likelihood that cooperative relations among southern African states would raise more risks than conflictual ones.

South Africa already has a large amount to say about exports of strategic minerals from southern Africa. It rests its case for support from the West in part on its reputation as a reliable supplier. One could argue that if South Africa had no security pressures, it might be willing to collude with its neighbors on supply and price. This argument rests less on the possibilities for regional cooperation and collusion in southern Africa than on a view with respect to the power and interests of a South Africa that did not feel threatened and did not need Western support, and thus could alter supply and price relationships. For the short, medium, and perhaps long runs, interstate and internal conflict rather than regional cooperation raise supply-interruption risks for strategic minerals.

At present, the depressed economies of southern Africa are in an especially weakened state and cannot hold supplies off markets. Drought has struck hard at Botswana and Zimbabwe (and at South Africa as well). Depressed copper prices have affected Zaire and Zambia, both dependent for their revenues on copper exports. Civil strife has been large scale in Angola and Mozambique. Zimbabwe, too, has been affected by ethnic and political conflict. Conflict has persisted in Namibia. In the economic and political climates that have existed, it has been difficult to attract significant new investment to most southern African states, although some large donor commitments were raised.[34] The U.S. Agency for International Development (USAID), for one, has believed that SADCC is worth supporting and that, although the resolution of political turmoil in southern Africa is essential for effective long-term development, enlarged and inventive development programs can ease political transitions and minimize damage to economies.[35]

Western donors have supported SADCC, but they have not protested effectively against South Africa's policies that have struck at the economies of the SADCC countries. South Africa's support for insurgency in Angola and Mozambique and the use of economic weapons against Lesotho and Zimbabwe have weakened the economies of these countries.[36] The effect of its destabilization policies has been to make southern African countries less attractive for investors and less able to focus on longer-range economic policies. The United States has supported both SADCC and a policy of constructive engagement with South Africa. Constructive engagement, however, has become perceived widely in Africa as a policy that gives South Africa a green light to weaken the very economies that aid to SADCC is meant to support.

A Cooperative Future?

It is debatable whether South Africa's policies have been designed to influence and to warn southern African countries and make them more sensitive to South Africa's security concerns, or whether South Africa wants weakened and unstable neighbors. South Africa has frequently denied that unstable neighbors are to its advantage.[37] When Mozambique became independent, South Africa stated its acceptance of that independence and would not permit local recruitment of mercenaries who might bid for power in Mozambique. Prime Minister Vorster insisted that what South Africa wanted was for Mozambique to be a country that would not allow itself to be used for attacks against South Africa and that would have a stable government.[38] What made Angola very different from Mozambique was that Angola had been used as a springboard for anti–South African actions in Namibia, that there was early Cuban and Soviet military involvement in Angola, that the Angolan anticolonial movement was split, and that South Africa had much more economic leverage to use against Mozambique than against Angola. Angola, of all the southern African states close to South Africa—excluding the geographically removed Tanzania—is least economically dependent on South Africa. Thus in order to exert political influence, South Africa required more direct military means. When South Africa perceived later that Mozambique was harboring South African insurgents, it was willing to take direct action.

Although South Africa has apparently not wanted to bring down the Machel regime in Mozambique, it has assisted the MNR insurgency. Toward Angola, on the other hand, South Africa has more complicated and varied motives: the removal of Cuban troops, the unwillingness so far to see a SWAPO regime in Namibia, and the unwillingness to abandon support for Jonas Savimbi of UNITA. One must ask whether the South Africans also hope for a friendly regime in Luanda, and one that would cooperate economically and politically with them. Posing this question raises two additional what-if questions. First, if South Africa were assured by its neighbors that their territories would not be used against South Africa for staging assaults and also that they would not actively oppose the homelands and separate-development policies, what would regional economic-development patterns look like? Second, if a regime were in power in South Africa that was not anathema to black African states, what would regional economic policies look like?

There is some uncertainty as to whether neighboring states will ever be able to satisfy South Africa that they will provide no safe haven for insurgents. Weak states in southern Africa often do not have complete control over their own countryside. Zimbabwean insurgents on Zambia's soil during the anti-Smith war were probably stronger than the Zambian army. Mozambique cannot put down the MNR insurgency. But even assuming that southern African states can and will comply with South Africa's wishes, by their very existence they are to some extent a challenge to doctrines of white supremacy. South Africa might not want their economic development to proceed smoothly. Surely it would want to retain important levers of economic control to maintain their economic dependence. There might well be more cooperation between South Africa and other southern African states; but, failing fundamental change within South Africa, this cooperation would continue to be limited and would be defined by the economic needs of southern African states on the one hand and South Africa's security concerns on the other.

If there were fundamental political changes in South Africa, southern African states still would not want to be dominated by a large, nearby power. They would look for economic relationships elsewhere in Africa, too, as well as among themselves. But southern African states are neither equally dependent on South Africa, nor do they all share common purposes, political systems, and outlooks. Their economies are hardly complementary, although Zimbabwe might in the future carry out some of the economic roles that South Africa now performs as a food exporter and manufacturing center. Just as southern African states would not want to be dominated by South Africa, even a black-led South Africa, they would not want to be dominated by Zimbabwe either. In Africa, customs unions and free-trade areas have been dominated by the strongest economy. Thus we could expect that southern African states will want to proliferate economic relationships if they can do so without prohibitive cost. In a friendly southern Africa, Zimbabwe might still move to fill certain trade roles that South Africa has dominated.

Tanzania has looked south for political reasons. Its politics has imposed certain economic costs on it, especially commitments to investment in transport facilities in order to help lessen Zambian dependence on South Africa and the former Rhodesia prior to Zimbabwe's independence. Tanzania's economic center of gravity would be once again oriented toward Kenya and Uganda if better political relations obtained in East Africa. Angola and Zaire might have more economic dealings, and

Zaire and Angola might both look to more extensive relations with Central African countries as well as with southern African ones if they were in more harmony with each other and had internal peace, which would facilitate the development of their economies in different parts of their countries.

Under all conditions of politics in southern Africa, the states of the region will be economically linked. Also under all conditions, however, they would try to delink from South Africa to some extent. A hostile South Africa gives greater incentive to the delinking for states for which this is a conceivable strategy: Zambia, Zimbabwe, and Mozambique.

One scheme for lessening Botswana's and Zimbabwe's transport dependence on South Africa involves a projected trans-Kalahari railroad. This project, however, which would be very expensive, also involves a projection of an independent Namibia, giving Zimbabwe and Botswana access to the Atlantic Ocean, and allowing Botswana to develop minerals in its western areas.[39]

New southern African road networks also envision construction through Namibia, but this would only lessen dependence on South Africa if Namibia becomes independent. Even then an independent Namibia would remain in South Africa's economic thrall. A SWAPO-ruled Namibia would be at least as vulnerable to South African–supported insurgency as Mozambique or Angola. Thus, even if more cooperation comes about between SADCC states and their economic ties grow, they will still be hostage to an unfriendly South Africa if there continues in the Republic a regime determined to maintain white supremacy. Nor will it be easy to create complementarities and division of labor among the SADCC economies. Even if SADCC emphasizes mutual benefit through project development, there is no quick fix for the problems of southern African economies and for their dependence on South Africa. Regional organizations cannot overcome ingrained structural difficulties.

Finally, the argument has been made that South Africa needs its hinterland for markets, unlimited labor, and investment opportunities. Without such access, it has been said, South Africa will begin to atrophy, as did Rhodesia.[40] This seems dubious reasoning. South Africa can draw on a large labor supply from its own homelands. It uses less migrant labor than in earlier years. Its trade with southern Africa is not large as a share of its world trade. Southern Africa will continue to require imports of food and manufacturing equipment, and South Africa will have comparative advantages in exporting to southern African states. Even if neighboring states should truly refuse to import from South Africa, that country can export outside of Africa. Moreover, southern African states will have to export through South Africa for many years.

South Africa would benefit from a cooperative future with southern

African states, and they would benefit also. But South Africa can continue to exist in a noncooperative, even hostile environment in southern Africa. Perhaps not all southern African regimes as now constituted can do the same. Southern African states can, and have to some extent, reoriented their economies away from South Africa.[41] But those economies can be damaged by punitive actions from the south.

Mutual economic benefits will not overcome political conflict in southern Africa in the sense that hostile states will come together for cooperative economic ventures that will then work to ameliorate political strife. Economic necessity does moderate the policies of southern African states toward South Africa. So far, economic necessities have not moderated the activities of South Africa toward its weaker neighbors. Perhaps it will occur in the future, but there is not much current evidence for such a prediction.

Notes

1. *World Development Report* (New York, 1983), 148–149. For recent trends in South Africa's economy, see U.S. Department of Commerce, International Trade Administration, *Foreign Economic Trends and Their Implications for the United States: South Africa* (Washington, D.C., 1983).

2. *Report,* 152–153.

3. Ibid., 158–159.

4. Ibid., 194–195.

5. See the International Institute for Strategic Studies, *The Military Balance 1983–84* (London, 1983), 66–81.

6. Power from Cahora Bassa, originating in Mozambique, goes through a South African station near Pretoria and then returns to Mozambique, even supplying Maputo. From 1980 Mozambiquan dissidents sabotaged the power lines to South Africa, depriving ESCOM and Mozambique of this source.

7. Report of the Study Commission on U.S. Policy toward Southern Africa, *South Africa: Time Running Out* (Berkeley, 1981), 290–291.

8. Ibid., 288.

9. Ibid.

10. *The Economist,* July 16, 1983, using South African Foreign Trade Office's statistics. Also see, for South Africa's economic relations with southern African states: Theo Malan, "Mozambique's and Zambia's Economic Relations with South Africa," *ISSUP Strategic Review* (January 1981), and various issues of the Economist Intelligence Unit's *Economic Reviews of Southern Africa.*

11. For discussion of the trade preference agreements between Zimbabwe and South Africa, see Larry Bowman, Michael Bratton, and Rudzo Murapa, "Zimbabwe and South Africa: Dependency, Destabilization and Liberation," in Thomas M. Callaghy (ed.), *South Africa in Southern Africa: The Intensifying Vortex of Violence* (New York, 1983), 341.

12. Owen Ellison Kahn, "South Africa and the Political Economy of Min-

erals in Southern Africa: The Case of Zimbabwe and Chromium," ibid., 97. See also Rotberg, "Introduction," above, 8–9.

13. For discussions of Zimbabwe's and Mozambique's dependence on South Africa for transport in order to export, see Bowman, Bratton, and Murapa, "Zimbabwe and South Africa"; and Thomas Callaghy, "Apartheid and Socialism: Southern Africa's Relations with Angola and Mozambique," in Callaghy, *Vortex*, 237–266.

14. Kenneth Grundy, "South Africa in the Political Economy of Southern Africa," in Gwendolen Carter and Patrick O'Meara (eds.), *International Politics in Southern Africa* (Bloomington, 1982), 168.

15. Study Commission, *South Africa: Time Running Out*, 291.

16. Callaghy, *Vortex*, 303.

17. Kenneth Grundy, "Economic Patterns in the New Southern African Balance," in Carter and O'Meara, *Southern Africa*, 308.

18. Bernard Magubane, "Botswana, Lesotho, and Swaziland: South Africa's Hostages in Revolt," in Callaghy, *Vortex*, 363.

19. For an early discussion of South Africa's economic and political dominance in a systematic set of relationships, see Larry Bowman, "The Subordinate State System of Southern Africa," *International Studies Quarterly*, XII (1968), 231–261.

20. Even membership in a technical organization such as the Southern African Regional Commission for the Conservation and Utilization of Soil (SARCCUS) was described as being important in the early 1970s for contact and influence as well as technical cooperation. See D.M. Joubert, "The Contribution of SARCCUS to Development and Cooperation in Southern Africa," *The South African Journal of African Affairs*, III (1973), 1–7, Zimbabwe left SARCUSS in October 1980.

21. Larry Bowman, "South Africa's Strategy and Its Implications for the United States," *International Affairs*, XLVII (1971), 25. According to Grundy, "Economic Patterns," 298, ESCOM originally did not want to buy Cahora Bassa electricity. Grundy maintains that ESCOM was pushed by the Department of Foreign Affairs and the South African Industrial Development Corporation to participate in Cahora Bassa.

22. Wolfgang Thomas, "The Economy in Transition to Independence," in Robert Rotberg (ed.), *Namibia: Political and Economic Prospects* (Lexington, Mass., 1983), 45.

23. For a statement of this linkage, see Eschel M. Rhoodie, "Southern Africa: Towards a New Commonwealth?" in Christian Potholm and Richard Dale (eds.), *Southern Africa in Perspective* (New York, 1972), 276–297.

24. A trade pact was signed with Malawi in 1968. South Africa established good relations with the Malagasy Republic at this time, and a large trade mission from South Africa went to Malagasy in 1969.

25. For a statement of the limits of South Africa's economic influence, see Grundy, "South Africa in the Political Economy," 151.

26. See Willie Breytenbach (ed.), *The Constellation of States: A Consideration* (Johannesburg, 1980).

27. A number of African leaders have openly met with South African leaders, however, including Presidents Kenneth Kaunda, Félix Houphouet-Boigny, and William Tolbert. Grundy, "South Africa," 157, points out how the con-

stellation-of-states concept is tied to domestic concerns. When Prime Minister Botha explained the underlying reasons for this framework, he emphasized the need to promote free enterprise and to resist the Marxist onslaught. See "Towards a Constellation of States in Southern Africa: Meeting between the Prime Minister and Business Leaders," Johannesburg, November 22, 1979, as found in Carter and O'Meara, *International Politics in Southern Africa*, 243.

28. On a number of occasions, President Kaunda has voiced the fear that a constellation of states would mean that southern African countries would become satellites or puppets of South Africa. See *Rand Daily Mail*, November 26, 1979, as found in Deon Geldenhuys, "South Africa's Regional Policy," in Michael Clough (ed.), *Changing Realities in Southern Africa* (Berkeley, 1982), 123–160. Geldenhuys reviews South Africa's regional policies very well, linking those policies to domestic concerns.

29. Study Commission, *South Africa: Time Running Out*, 294. It has also been argued that a constellation of states might move South Africa to internal reforms and/or create more rather than less economic balance in the region. These do not seem to be the ideas that are widely shared in southern Africa.

30. It has been argued that the origins of SADCC can be traced to the group of frontline states, founded in 1974 to pursue independence for Zimbabwe. Indeed, some would push the origins of SADCC back to the Conference of East and Central African Heads of State, in Nairobi in 1966, where regional cooperation and liberation in southern Africa were discussed. See Michael Clough and John Ravenhill, "Regional Cooperation in Southern Africa: The Southern African Development Coordination Conference," in Clough, *Changing Realities*, 162.

31. Various aims include upgrading port facilities in Beira, Nacala, Maputo (Mozambique), Lobito (Angola), and Dar es Salaam (Tanzania). South African states look toward a time when Walvis Bay might be a west coast outlet for Zambia and Botswana, and possibly for Zimbabwe when rail links between Francistown and Gobabis become economically feasible. Of course this presumes that Walvis Bay is not controlled by South Africa. Reopening and upgrading the Benguela railroad and assisting the Tazara railroad to become more efficient also are anticipated. Linking Malawi to the Zambian border via rail and through Lake Malawi into the Tazara system has also been discussed. Zaire, which is not a SADCC member, is brought into the discussion on rail networks.

32. Study Commission, *South Africa: Time Running Out*, 445.

33. I do not want to rehash these debates. For fuller presentations of the analyses that argue that U.S. and Western vulnerability is not critical in the short run and that long-run policies for stockpiling, new sources, and new technologies and substitution can be developed, see Robert S. Jaster, *Southern Africa in Conflict: Implications for U.S. Policies in the 1980s* (Washington, D.C., 1982); Study Commission, *South Africa: Time Running Out*, 310–322; Robert Perlman and Anthony Murray, "Resources and Conflict: Requirements and Vulnerabilities of the Industrialized World," *Third World Conflict and International Security*, (London, 1981); Michael Shafer, "Mineral Myths," *Foreign Policy* XLVII (1982), 154–171; U.S. Senate, Committee on Foreign Relations, Subcommittee on African Affairs, "Imports of Minerals from South Africa by the U.S. and the OECD Countries" (Washington, D.C., 1980).

For analyses that argue that there is a strategic threat to the United States resulting from problems of access to resources, see Council on Economics and National Security, *Strategic Minerals: A Resource Crisis* (New Brunswick, N.J., 1980); Walter F. Hahn and Alvin J. Cottrell, *Soviet Shadow over Africa* (Coral Gables, Fla., 1976); Ministry of Information, Embassy of South Africa, "South Africa: Persian Gulf of Minerals" (Washington, D.C., 1980); Daniel S. Mariaschin, "Soviet Union Is on the Move: It Fights Western Control of Strategic Raw Materials," *Los Angeles Times,* February 13, 1981.

Useful general analyses include: U.N. Centre of Transnational Corporations, *The Activities of Transnational Corporations in the Industrial, Mining, and Military Sectors of Southern Africa* (New York, 1980); William N. Raiford, *The European Role in Africa and U.S. Interests* (Washington, D.C., 1981). Specifically on South Africa's impact on Zimbabwe's chrome exports, see Kahn, "Political Economy of Minerals," 69–106.

34. Western states and international organizations and development banks pledged $65 million to SADCC in 1980, although much of this was a renewal of bilateral loans and aid pledged earlier. Annual investment in South Africa runs about ten times the total for the nine southern African states. Negative annual rates of investment occurred in Angola, Mozambique, and Zambia between 1970 and 1979. See Jeremy Ben-Ami, "United States Economic Policy towards Southern Africa," Woodrow Wilson School, Princeton University, unpub. paper, 1983.

35. In 1977 the U.S. Congress requested USAID to undertake a comprehensive analysis of the development needs of southern Africa to determine what contributions U.S. assistance could make. USAID recruited Roy Stacey, who had been on the Club du Sahel Secretariat, to lead the U.S. effort.

36. One assessment of damage to Angola's infrastructure since 1975 is $7 billion. *The Economist,* July 16, 1983, p. 21. Of course, the cost is from civil war, not just from South Africa's actions.

37. However, *The Economist,* July 16, 1983, p. 28, says that South Africa's strategists talk of a "shield of instability" in southern Africa and the "Lebanonization" of Angola, Mozambique, and Zimbabwe.

38. Geldenhuys, "South Africa's Regional Policy," 142.

39. Clough and Ravenhill, "Regional Cooperation," 182.

40. Grundy, "Economic Patterns in the New Southern African Balance," 312.

41. Dependence can increase, too. Mozambique's food imports from South Africa almost tripled between 1979 and 1981. The Rhodesian war for independence worked to increase Zambia's dependence on South Africa.

6
Squaring Up to Economic Dominance: Regional Patterns

Gavin G. Maasdorp

A s the 1970s drew to a close, the frontline states—Zambia, Botswana, Tanzania, Angola, and Mozambique—considered forming a regional organization to promote economic development and resolve conflicts. Background research was commissioned and papers were prepared in 1977 and 1978; these were later presented to a conference in Arusha, Tanzania, in 1979 at which a declaration of intent also was approved. This was ratified in Lusaka in April 1980, when the five countries, together with Malawi, Lesotho, Swaziland, and the newly independent Zimbabwe, formally established the Southern African Development Coordination Conference (SADCC) (see figure 6–1).[1]

Concurrent with this initiative of the frontline states were efforts to establish two further economic groupings involving countries in the region—namely, the South African government's proposal for a Constellation of Southern African States (CONSAS) and the Preferential Trade Area for Eastern and Southern Africa (officially PTAESA, but usually abbreviated to PTA), which was promoted by the United Nations Economic Commission for Africa.

Pretoria envisaged that CONSAS would comprise all of Africa south of the Kunene and Zambezi rivers, but the possibility of extending it to embrace other countries in the region was not discounted. The idea was rebuffed by neighboring countries, however, and thus CONSAS consists merely of South Africa and the four "independent" homelands—that is, a restructuring within the 1910 boundaries of the Union of South Africa. In contrast, the PTA extends beyond the confines of the subcontinent. It was formally inaugurated in 1983 with headquarters in Lusaka. The position in 1984 was that of the twenty potential members, ten (Djibouti, Ethiopia, Kenya, Lesotho, Malawi, Mauritius, Somalia, Uganda, Zambia, and Zimbabwe) had both signed and ratified the treaty; four (Burundi, the Comoros, Rwanda, and Swaziland) had signed but not ratified; and six (Angola, Botswana, Madagascar, Mozambique, Seychelles, and

Figure 6–1. SADCC Countries

Tanzania) had yet to sign. Thus only five of the nine SADCC states had joined the PTA (see figure 6–2).

SADCC has an institutional structure that includes a summit of heads of state, a council of ministers, sectoral commissions, and a secretariat headed by a secretary-general and located in Gaborone. Responsibility for coordination action in the priority areas identified by SADCC is allocated among the nine countries as follows: Angola (energy); Botswana (crop research and animal disease control); Lesotho (soil conservation and land utilization); Malawi (fisheries, forestry, and wildlife); Mozambique (transport and communications); Swaziland (manpower); Tanzania (industry); Zambia (development fund and mining); and Zimbabwe (food security). Funding for projects is obtained from donors (international agencies and individual countries). An annual consultative meeting is held with these international partners, and the emphasis to date has been on transportation and communications and agriculture, and latterly also on industry and energy.

Jargon aside, SADCC has set out to pursue, through coordinated action, the following goals:

1. To reduce economic dependence, especially on South Africa.
2. To promote regional cooperation and the equitable sharing of the benefits of that cooperation.
3. To mobilize the resources of member countries to promote national, interstate, and regional policies for economic development.
4. To secure international support for its strategy and aid for its projects.

The crucial questions are whether SADCC will be able (1) to survive intact as an economic grouping, (2) to reduce the dependence of its members on South Africa and (3) to reach a lasting political accord with Pretoria that allows economic development to proceed under conditions of relative peace.

The Future: Survival or Stress?

Attempts at regional economic cooperation throughout the world have a checkered history. Africa has been no exception, and SADCC has attracted its share of skeptics. Whether or not this skepticism is justified can be determined only by an examination of forces that may be binding or dividing, either now or in the future.

Figure 6–2. PTA Countries

Common Interests

The SADCC countries perceive a number of common interests. First, like the rest of the Third World, they wish to promote economic development and reduce their dependence on richer countries. Although each country obviously has its own national policy, the countries have to work together on certain issues, transport cooperation between maritime and landlocked states being an obvious case. But all are relatively small and weak individually, and therefore there is considerable merit in establishing a regional grouping to bargain with the rest of the world. The same argument may be applied to their positions vis-à-vis South Africa; table 6–1 illustrates South Africa's overwhelming economic strength in the subcontinent. An economic grouping of the less-developed countries would therefore enable some of them, at any rate, to reduce the extent of their dependence on South Africa by diversifying their external links.

Although the emphasis is on common economic interests, there is also a common political interest, namely, opposition to the race policies of South Africa. This is an emotional issue that cements ties elsewhere in Africa.

A number of other points are also relevant. SADCC is not a legacy of colonialism; it is a voluntary association and has not been imposed from outside. The bureaucracy has been kept to a minimum, in part through the spreading of sectoral responsibilities among the countries. Finally, the scope of activities is limited to areas in which the benefits from cooperation are easily discernible.[2]

Table 6–1
Population, National Product, and Per Capita Income, SADCC Countries and South Africa, 1980

Country	Population (millions)	GNP ($ millions)	GNP per capita ($)
Botswana	0.8	730	910
Lesotho	1.3	520	390
Swaziland	0.6	380	680
Mozambique	12.1	2810	230
Angola	7.1	3320	470
Zambia	5.8	3220	560
Zimbabwe	7.4	4640	630
Malawi	6.1	1390	230
Tanzania	18.7	4780	280
Total SADCC	59.9	21,490	359
South Africa	1.0	66,960	2,290
Note: Namibia =	1.0	1,420	1,410

Source: *African Insight* 13(8), 1983.

Theoretical Justification

Membership in SADCC does not exclude states from participation in other economic groupings; for example, Botswana, Lesotho, and Swaziland (BLS) remain in the Southern African Customs Union (SACU) with South Africa. SADCC is a loose association and therefore avoids most of the difficulties inherent in economic-integration arrangements such as free-trade areas and customs unions.

Theoretically, a country should enter into economic-integration arrangements only with others at similar levels of development.[3] This is clearly not the case in southern Africa (see Table 6–1); the point can be illustrated by referring to the existing Customs Union.[4]

At first glance, in terms of theory, it might seem absurd that small states such as the BLS ones are in a customs union with a larger, more industrially developed country. On closer examination, however, one can explain why the SACU has been unusually successful and harmonious. First, an income-raising factor in the revenue-sharing formula, together with a stabilization factor, are attractive to BLS. Second, South Africa is the cheapest source of basic consumer goods for their low-income populations. Yet the customs union also contains disadvantages: The BLS countries have found it difficult to industrialize, partly because they have a limited domestic-market potential and partly because they find it difficult to compete against more efficient South African industries. Their small economic size, moreover, limits the potential for such competition, and therefore they probably have less to lose from preferential-trade relationships with South Africa than would other countries in SADCC. Because they have larger populations, the other SADCC members have a greater potential for import-substituting industries and hence more to lose from competition with South African industries. Consequently, they would almost certainly find closer economic ties (such as those envisaged in CONSAS) less attractive.

Yet official SADCC communiques repeatedly have stated that South Africa would be welcomed as a member if it were to change its domestic policies: President Kaunda has even gone on record as saying that a racially integrated South Africa would be welcome in the PTA as well.[5] These statements imply that SADCC's problem with South Africa is political rather than economic; the stated goal of reducing dependence on South Africa then is shown up as stemming from an opposition to apartheid rather than from any real or imagined problems of dependence in themselves. More important, however, these statements have to be examined from the perspective of economic theory relating to integration and trade.

Although SADCC is not an economic-integration arrangement, it is an attempt to promote trade among its members, albeit along informal lines. Should it formalize preferential-trade agreements among its members, however, then it is difficult to see how South Africa could be welcomed into such an organization as its exports would be likely to overwhelm the SADCC market if tariff barriers were to be lowered. The only way for SADCC to admit South Africa to membership under preferential-trade conditions, and at the same time to avoid having its markets dominated, would be to wring concessions out of Pretoria; an example is the preferential-trade agreement between South Africa and Zimbabwe, which heavily favors the latter's products. The problem, however, is that certain industries in South Africa already are strongly opposed to the terms of the Zimbabwean agreement. Opposition to an extension on concessionary terms of such an agreement to the entire SADCC area would emanate from a wide spectrum of the manufacturing sector; in such circumstances Pretoria hardly would be able to negotiate membership. In short, SADCC's theoretical attitude to a racially integrated South Africa may be summed up as follows: normal trade—yes; concessionary preferential trade—yes; preferential trade on equal terms— no, even were a black radical government to be installed in Pretoria.[6] In other words, the formation of SADCC then would be justified on theoretical economic grounds quite irrespective of politics.

Another important focus of SADCC's activities relates to the coordination of industrial development among member countries. This entails the allocation of industrial plants among members. In practice it is extremely difficult to obtain agreement on allocations, and again the process would be unlikely to prove easier if South Africa were to be admitted to the grouping. South Africa has a difficult enough task to create manufacturing jobs on a scale sufficient to keep its own unemployment down to manageable proportions, without the added complication of having to conform to an outside allocation of new industries.

The question of relationships with South Africa aside, and given the fact that the nine countries wish to cooperate economically, is there a theoretical justification for the formation of SADCC?

Recent work on economic integration is critical of formal schemes. Thus El-Agraa finds that the theory fails to provide an economic rationale for the formation of customs unions,[7] whereas Robson concludes that "no *a priori* case exists for integration among developing countries,"[8] and Green considers the theory "largely irrelevant to the actual purposes, processes and problems of Third World economic coordination."[9]

From a theoretical point of view, therefore, SADCC would seem to be superior both to the PTA, which is regarded as merely the first step toward full integration, and to the SACU. This advantage over the PTA may prove decisive in determining the long-term future of the two organizations; but, for the reasons mentioned above, the BLS countries derive certain advantages from the SACU not normally found in economic-integration schemes.

Problems

Nevertheless, establishing a rationale for the existence of SADCC does not necessarily mean that the grouping will function effectively. SADCC is aware that there are problems that have to be overcome in "building up the habit of effective regional co-ordination."[10] At the same time, however, it is sensitive to the tendency of commentators to concentrate on what it sees as divisive issues and to cast doubts about its ability to succeed.[11] However, precisely because, in the light of past schemes that have failed, it is easier to document the obstacles (present and potential) than the binding factors, it is important to examine such problems in order to determine their magnitude and likely effect.

The success of SADCC will depend on the following:

1. The maintenance of political goodwill among members.
2. The maintenance of political stability in member countries.
3. The efficient operation of sectoral responsibilities, especially of transport services.
4. An equitable distribution of the benefits of membership.
5. An ability to attract funds greater than that of countries acting individually.

Political Goodwill. At the outset, an obvious problem is that the SADCC states are a disparate lot. They differ in the degree of their economic ties with South Africa, their colonial background, their present ideologies, and the state of their economies.

So far as their economic links with Pretoria are concerned, at one extreme Botswana, Lesotho, and Swaziland are partners in the Southern African Customs Union, whereas Lesotho and Swaziland are fellow members of the Rand Monetary Area (RMA). The Southern African Regional Tourist Council (SARTOC) embraces Malawi, Swaziland, and South Africa. There is some trade between Angola and South Africa and even less in the case of Tanzania, which historically has been more closely oriented to East rather than southern Africa, having been part of the East African Common Market with Kenya and Uganda. The remaining members have strong links with Pretoria in one or more of the transport, trade, and employment fields.

Angola and Mozambique are former Portuguese territories; the remaining countries in the grouping are part of the British Commonwealth.

Angola, Mozambique, Tanzania, Zambia, and Zimbabwe are following various socialist policies of development, whereas the others adhere to the market-economy path.

The countries have chalked up vastly differing economic performances since their independence. Although Malawi, Botswana, and Swaziland were achieving favorable rates of economic growth until they encountered adverse conditions not of their own making in the 1980s, the economies of Tanzania and Zambia are run down, and those of Angola and Mozambique have deteriorated rapidly. Zimbabwe is experiencing the political, social, and economic problems of reorganization after a civil war, as well as the problems stemming from adapting to a new economic system. No fewer than four of the SADCC countries—Lesotho, Malawi, Tanzania, and Angola—are classified as "least developed"; that is, they are among the world's poorest nations.

These contrasts have led Weisfelder to state that "only exceptional circumstances and ingenuity can sustain solidarity within so diverse a group,"[12] and both he and Thompson conclude that the combining of different economic systems in SADCC could create serious problems.[13] For example, there may be conflicts between efficiency and economic growth, on the one hand, and equity and localization, on the other; or the countries may have different priorities for investment—for example, telecommunications versus rural development. These differences could easily create problems in the way of cooperating on projects; in short, SADCC may become bogged down "in a host of squabbles rooted in divergent approaches to developmental problems."[14]

In the past, differing foreign policies within the grouping have caused some tension. This issue first came to the fore at the Maputo consultative meeting in 1980, when it became clear that ideological differences were frustrating certain projects. Because Angola and Mozambique are not signatories to the Lomé II Convention, projects located in these countries do not qualify to receive EEC aid; and this caused concern among the remaining seven, which are signatories. Subsequently, however, both countries indicated their willingness to participate in the next round of the Lomé talks in 1983. The position at present, therefore, is that the EEC cannot fund key port and rail projects in Angola and Mozambique, but that the two countries nevertheless qualify for some EEC funds available for nonassociates of the Lomé Convention.

This change in attitude by Angola and Mozambique has been interpreted as "a tacit admission that the Communist Comecon trade bloc cannot meet their development requirements."[15] Comecon is an association of industrialized countries, and it finds it difficult to integrate Third World countries. Thus Angola has adopted a more pragmatic attitude toward the West, especially with regard to investment. Mozambique also is mending its fences with the West and has established diplomatic relations with the United States.

Thus foreign-policy differences appear to have diminished, even though Angola is still ideologically close to the Comecon grouping. SADCC has rejected the idea of a formal alliance between itself as an organization and the major power blocs.

Political Stability. *Political stability* here refers to the functioning of a political system free of armed aggression on the part of dissident groups against an existing government. Clearly, the existence of such aggression could hamper the ability of any particular country to fulfill its obligations to SADCC, and could also threaten SADCC projects in that country.

There is a wide range of political systems within the grouping—from a multiparty parliamentary democracy in Botswana to one-party states of the left and right. It is in some of these one-party states that instability is found—notably in Angola and Mozambique, where guerrilla activities damage transportation links. The causes of instability have been partly external—destabilization by outside powers, which will be discussed later—and partly internal in the sense that acts of aggression are bound to occur in countries where there is no freedom of political association or expression.

Guerrilla activities in Angola and Mozambique have had a severe impact on SADCC transport projects. SADCC has made transport its key sector because of the dependence of most of its members on the South African network. Within the transport sector, the emphasis is on the east coast ports—especially those of Mozambique—and associated rail and road projects. Given that Mozambique is assigned the key strategic role, it stands to reason that political stability within that country is a sine qua non for the reduction of SADCC dependence on the South African network. However, its transport system has been the target of frequent attacks by the Mozambique National Resistance (MNR).[16] For the landlocked countries, therefore, transport links through Mozambique have proved fragile.

From the end of 1983 the Beira-Maputo road and the Beira-Malawi and Maputo-Zimbabwe railways were virtually unusable. In 1985, a year after the Nkomati Accord, the question still is: Just how temporary is the problem? Can the government of Mozambique defeat the MNR?

The disruption of key transport links has the potential to disturb political relationships within SADCC, and this potential is exacerbated by the inefficient operation of railways and ports.

Efficient Sectoral Operations. The problem of inefficiency in Mozambique is most marked in the transport sector. It has been said that the guerrilla activities of the MNR probably cause fewer problems than the continued poor management of ports and railways in Mozambique as well as the shortage of specialists and materials to effect repairs.

A main reason is the chronic shortage of middle management caused by a combination of several factors—the neglect of African education and training prior to independence, the adoption after independence of an ideology that induced most of the existing skilled manpower to leave the country, an unwillingness on the part of government to engage large numbers of expatriates on contract, and a reluctance among expatriates to accept postings to a country suffering from an uncertain security position as well as chronic shortages of foodstuffs and other consumer goods. Added to this is the difficulty of improving productivity levels in the local labor force when the local currency is almost worthless and there is nothing to buy with higher earnings.[17]

Similar problems have occurred on the Tazara rail line between Tanzania and Zambia, but both governments have realized that they were too hasty in localizing posts and thus 250 Chinese managerial and technical staff returned to Africa at the end of 1983. The position on Tazara has improved, but concern has been expressed about the ability of the Zimbabwean railway system to cope with traffic in view of resignations of key managerial staff and an increase in accidents.[18]

The combined effect of guerrilla attacks and inefficiency is to slow the movement of cargo, and the success of SADCC may depend on the political willingness of member states to accept this fact. However, inefficiency also may arise through the administrative structure of SADCC and the allocation of sectoral responsibilities among member countries.

The fact that SADCC is not a large bureaucracy—it has only a small secretariat in Gaborone and is represented abroad by a liaison committee in London—is regarded both by the grouping itself and by some commentators as an advantage. In contrast, other writers believe this structuring may prove disadvantageous.

Apparently, there was considerable pressure to have a large secretariat, but doing so was resisted—notably by Botswana, which has an efficient civil service and was reluctant to see the creation of a large bureaucracy for fear that it would degenerate into a talking shop. Now, however, there is concern about SADCC's capacity to shoulder a growing burden of project implementation. Countries responsible for sectoral coordination are free to approach their responsibilities as they think best. The only commission established thus far is in the transport and communications sector. For the rest, technical units usually are set up within the relevant ministry in the coordinating country—for example, the ministry of energy in Angola and the ministry of industries in Tanzania—whereas in the ministry of agriculture in Zimbabwe there is a four-person

Dual load

administrative support unit. These arrangements mean that government officials in those countries may shoulder a dual load—their normal national work plus SADCC responsibilities. These technical units probably strain the manpower resources of the coordinating countries anyway (unless they are staffed by specially recruited expatriates). As the number of projects increases, so does the burden on officials, whose capacity fully to utilize the funds and assistance promised has been questioned.[19]

quote Secretariat

The secretariat plays a coordinating role, assisting the ministries concerned in implementing their sectoral mandates. It arranges access to consultants for feasibility studies, and to technical experts, for whom it also may draw up conditions of service. Clearly, a major function of the secretariat is to implement decisions taken at summit meetings. The Zambian prime minister is reported to have criticized the way in which such decisions were being followed up: Financing bodies would not be prepared to invest in SADCC projects if they were not properly appraised, documented, and implemented; and donors had complained of undue delays in the use of funds allocated.[20]

No Bureaucracy power problem

lack of skilled people

Thus both the secretariat and the individual ministries may be understaffed. Indeed, at a press conference at Maseru, the secretary-general mentioned that one of the major problems facing SADCC was a shortage of skilled and experienced personnel to handle the various sectoral portfolios. This problem is aggravated by the multiplicity of meetings—with donors, at standing committees of officials, at summits, and so on. To quote Anglin: ". . . the proliferation in the number and frequency of specialised meetings has been so rapid that the burden of representation, in terms of money and manpower, is proving more than some governments can manage. As a result, there are already complaints of meetings having to be cancelled for lack of a quorum."[21]

Another factor that may strain the patience of some countries has been mentioned by Weisfelder. Referring to the allocation of responsibilities among the member states, he writes: "The probability that all SADCC states will sustain high involvement and fulfill their commitments to the organization is quite low. . . . Someone skeptical about SADCC once remarked that it required a special sense of humor to assign responsibility for development finance to Zambia and industrialization to Tanzania."[22] The problem is that a country does not necessarily have a record of achievement in the field for which it is allocated responsibility, and indeed it is not clear precisely how the allocations were made.[23]

Tanzania fucks up

Tanzania's presentation on industry was criticized at both the Blantyre and Maseru meetings. The 1983 report was regarded by delegates as neither well-researched nor realistic,[24] and the allocation of that sector as an act of cynicism on the part of the other members, given Tanzania's failure in the field and the disavowal of industrialization in its developmental planning.[25] Similarly, the quality of Zambia's work on the proposal to establish a development fund has been criticized at SADCC meetings. But a country does have recourse to technical assistance—the ECA has helped Zambia in its role—and this would not seem to be an insuperable problem.

Sharing of Benefits. This is another important internal problem facing the SADCC, and is linked with the issue of the emergence within the grouping of industrial polarization.

An equitable distribution of the costs and benefits of membership, though considered of critical importance in the theory of economic integration, is very difficult to achieve in practice. Failure to do so was one of the important reasons for the breakup of the East African Common Market. In particular, it is difficult to coordinate industrial development and distribute new plants among member states, and an official of the Confederation of Zimbabwean Industries has been quoted as saying that there is in-fighting with regard to industrial projects.[26] A degree of industrial polarization exists within the grouping—the nine countries are at different levels of industrial development, and this poses problems in the formulation of strategy for the sector. Zimbabwe is the most advanced industrial country and, like Kenya in the East African case, stands to increase its industrial dominance over time. There is already a realization of this fact; Weisfelder quotes top officials in Lesotho expressing their fears that SADCC may become a vehicle for Zimbabwean regional dominance,[27] and it has been said that Botswana is not keen to escape from the South African frying pan only to land in the Zimbabwean fire.[28] This problem manifested itself with the expected termination of preferential trade between Zimbabwe and South Africa in 1982. Since Zimbabwe was selling 75 percent of its manufactured goods south of the Limpopo River, it would clearly have had to find alternative markets, and it therefore looked to SADCC. But the individual states wanted to protect their own producers of similar goods—something they are entitled to do since SADCC is not a free-trade area. Recently, prominent Zimbabwean industrialists have stated that their country's industries are well placed to serve SADCC.[29] Statements of this kind only heighten the suspicion on the part of the other countries, although Weisfelder says that SADCC is aware that projects must be initiated quickly in all member states to forestall fears that only some are benefiting.[30] More recently, the then secretary-general implored Zimbabwe to see "the region not only as a market but as a possible source of essential imports."[31]

However, Zimbabwe has restricted clothing imports from Botswana and banned imports of rice from Malawi (its traditional supplier), instead purchasing 6,000 tons from North Korea.[32] In addition, Zimbabwe also has been involved in a controversy regarding energy.

The desire of countries to be self-sufficient in certain fields may militate against coordinated projects. For instance, a SADCC electricity grid is a technical possibility and would be of great economic advantage, provided that the countries trusted one another. However, countries tend to be very sensitive in energy matters; they are afraid of the damage that could be caused to their supplies if political relations change. They therefore attempt to become independent in the supply of electricity.[33] The point is taken, but if a SADCC electricity grid is to be established, member countries will have to take some risks and resist the temptation so common in the Third World to embark on prestige projects.

In 1982 Zimbabwe decided to proceed with the second stage of the Hwange (Wankie) power project. This would reduce its dependence on Zambia for power, but Zambia would lose its only major export to Zimbabwe. Zambia regarded doing so as contrary to the spirit of SADCC cooperation: It would have been cheaper for Zimbabwe to import hydroelectricity, and Zambia's foreign-exchange earnings then would have provided a market for a range of manufactured goods from Zimbabwe. Zambia's installed power capacity is double its domestic demand; but Zimbabwe, in pursuance of an energy strategy formulated during the Unilateral Declaration of Independence (UDI) period, has identified four hydroelectric sites on the Zambezi River and seven coalfields. From a SADCC point of view, it would be preferable for the installed capacity of Zambia and Mozambique to be used than to construct new plants.[34]

When asked whether Zimbabwe's policy accorded with that of SADCC, the then secretary-general of SADCC provided a diplomatic answer, but one that underlines an extremely important point: SADCC's regional strategy cannot prevent members from embarking on national programs.[35] SADCC merely strives to coordinate these national plans in order to strengthen development in a regional context, but it has no power to check or reduce gaps between member states or to compensate the weaker ones.

Quite apart from nationalism, however, national economic policies have an important effect on the ability to attract foreign investment. As Kenya so amply has demonstrated, a country following a market-economy path with a minimum of bureaucratic red tape can create a climate conducive to private investment. Some SADCC countries follow contrary policies, although rapid decisions apparently can be made in Angola and Mozambique. In contrast, businessmen regard Tanzania as "offering investment disincentives."[36]

Attraction of Funds. The precise expectations that each of the nine countries entertained upon forming SADCC probably varied. However, the expectation of economic benefit almost certainly was a common one.

Thus another condition for the success of SADCC would seem to be that it must demonstrate that it is able to attract more funds than would its member states acting individually. It is not so easy to do so; for example, although the 1980 meeting in Maputo attracted pledges of $650 million, less than one-fifth of this sum could be considered new funds. The balance consisted of funds already committed by donors to individual countries, and it was convenient to donors to channel the existing aid through SADCC.

In principle, projects serving more than one country should be attractive to donors, but in practice donors have always preferred bilateral to multilateral aid. This reality is true both for Western and Comecon countries; both sides attach strings to aid funds and look for trade concessions. Not only are the Soviet-bloc countries parsimonious when it comes to foreign aid, but they have been described as "the most obsessive proponents of bilateralism within the SADCC experience,"[37] hence the absence of their support at the annual consultative meetings. Thus Angola and Mozambique probably would be able to negotiate more aid bilaterally than through SADCC (although any such aid from Comecon sources presumably would not be directed toward SADCC projects). It has yet to be shown that SADCC is more attractive for donors than is the continuation of bilateral aid to individual countries.

If individual countries negotiate aid funds themselves, to nail the projects concerned to the SADCC mast is to obscure the true position. In transport, for example, relatively little new funding has been negotiated by SADCC; most is from national sources or bilateral agreements that have been lumped under the organization's banner. The new funding that SADCC has obtained is for technical assistance and consultancy.

More important than securing pledges from donors, however, may be the successful functioning of the proposed Southern African Development Bank. It has a particularly important role with respect to the provision of foreign exchange. Some member states suffer from a shortage of foreign exchange to pay for goods and services and not only do these shortages restrict intra-SADCC trade, but they can sometimes prove sources of conflict. For example, Zambia was short of foreign exchange and accumulated huge arrears for port charges at Dar-es-Salaam, for which it was unable to pay. Thus its relations with Tanzania were soured.[38] The development of a payments mechanism by central banks may be essential to promote trade among member states, and a feasibility study of a clearing house is to be conducted.

The Future: Diminishing Dependence on South Africa?

The second important question regarding the future is the extent to which SADCC will be able to reduce its dependence on South Africa and the time scale likely to be involved. As we have noted, this reduction is one of SADCC's major aims; we have seen, too, that the perceived problem of dependence is essentially political (arising from South Africa's race policies) rather than economic. But dependence is artificial in the field in which it is greatest—namely, transport: South African ports are not the natural or traditional outlets for the landlocked countries north of the Limpopo. Dependence is economically undesirable in the spheres of food supplies and employment, the latter of course also presenting the political and social complications of racial discrimination. In the other major field of dependence—trade—the fact is that SADCC countries have to engage in international trade anyway, and the economic question is: Which goods can be obtained from which country at the lowest total delivery cost?

Transport

South Africa has 75 percent of the subcontinental rail network (figure 6–3) and the most efficient ports. Its rail system has traditionally carried most of the import traffic of the BLS countries and the export traffic of Botswana and Lesotho. However, because guerrilla warfare effectively has closed the railway from Zambia to the Angolan port of Lobito to international traffic for over eight years, and because of the insecurity and inefficiency (mentioned earlier) of the Mozambiquan transport system, South Africa has been handling an increasing proportion of the foreign trade of Zimbabwe, Zambia, and Zaire in the past few years. Although the volume conveyed has recently declined, it was estimated that in late 1983 some 65–70 percent of Zimbabwe's and 50–60 percent of Malawi's foreign trade was being routed via South Africa.[39] Comparative figures in the case of Zambia were 40 percent for exports and 70 percent for imports.

Factors that have prompted the switch in traffic from Mozambique include insecurity, organizational inefficiency, transport delays, the danger of theft, and poor telecommunications. Many of these factors are structural and will no doubt persist in the short term, but they could be overcome in the longer term—for example, through technical training. More problematical, however, is the security issue. South Africa often has been accused of supporting MNR attacks on roads, railways, and the oil pipeline in Mozambique in order to maintain its hold on SADCC traffic.[40] There have been military changes since Nkomati, however; the question today is whether MNR activities can be curbed.

If not, it is possible that the west coast ports may become a viable alternative to the east coast ones so far as the landlocked states are concerned, *provided* an internationally acceptable political settlement is

Figure 6–3. Southern African Rail Networks

achieved in Namibia *and* South Africa agrees to hand over Walvis Bay (which would be the terminus of the proposed trans-Kalahari railway). Even if South Africa retained its control of that port, a settlement probably would imply the withdrawal of all foreign forces from Angola and an eventual end to political instability (one way or the other), in which case Lobito and possibly other Angolan ports might assume greater importance, especially for Zambia. Lobito is the terminus of the Benguela railway, which was the main route for copper exports from Zambia and Zaire and for imports from the West.

Alternatively, the Tazara line might be able to cater for traffic from Zambia, Malawi, and possibly Zimbabwe; but this would depend on greatly improved rail and port management in Tanzania and on a further connection to Malawi, and would be enormously expensive for Zimbabwe. The Tazara line was opened in October 1975, two months after the effective closing to Zambia of the Rhodesian railway, and soon became the main route for Zambian traffic. But with the normalization of relations between Zambia and Zimbabwe in 1980, the southern route was reopened so that Zambia's traffic was once again redirected. In the last few years the Tazara line has operated under severe technical and managerial constraints but nevertheless has the potential capacity to carry all Zambia's external traffic, and Dar-es-Salaam is closer to the Copperbelt than either Lobito or Beira.[41]

Of all the SADCC countries, Malawi probably has been hardest hit by transport difficulties in Mozambique. Malawi has no rail link with Zambia and hence none with the Tazara line to Dar-es-Salaam, but recently signed an agreement with Tanzania to construct a road link between the countries to open up access to Tanzania's ports.[42]

In the meantime, however, in the absence of a direct rail connection, Malawian trade is obliged to use a combination of road and rail to and from South African ports. This difficulty adds to the already considerable increase in transport costs, and Malawi has found its competitive position on world markets for its major exports eroded, while an increased import bill (especially for fuel and fertilizer) has also been influential in forcing the country to renegotiate its external debt.[43]

In summary, the dependence of Zambia, Malawi, and Zimbabwe on the South African transport system could be eliminated *if* the rail and port systems of SADCC maritime states were to function efficiently and the existing infrastructure were to be improved. The first condition is dependent, in part at least, on security problems being overcome. At this stage there appears to be little hope of natural flows through Angola and Mozambique occurring for the next few years; in the meantime, Zambian and some Malawian traffic might be diverted to Dar-es-Salaam.

The remaining SADCC countries traditionally have had close transport links with South Africa. The southern railway system in Mozambique and the port of Maputo largely depend on traffic from the Witwatersrand, and one of the main thrusts of the Nkomati Accord is to reinforce this dependence. Although Maputo also is the natural port for Swaziland, the kingdom will be more than ever integrated with the South African system when a new northern rail link to Komatipoort is built. This project will increase the degree of interdependence between the countries: The finances of the Swaziland railway will depend heavily on mineral through-traffic from the Transvaal to Richards Bay, and the route will afford such traffic a considerable saving in transport costs.

Botswana also is to construct a new rail link to South Africa; and it is ironic, given the expressed SADCC objective of reducing transport links with South Africa, that the Botswana railway will depend for most of its revenue on attracting through-traffic between northern countries (notably Zambia and Zaire) and South Africa—that is, on *increasing* traffic flows to and from the south. Lesotho is totally dependent on South Africa in the field of transport and has no alternative given its geographical position.

Trade

The second important area of contact between South Africa and SADCC is trade. No detailed breakdown of South Africa's trade with the rest of the continent is available, but apart from exports of R1 billion within the customs union to the BLS countries, South Africa in 1981 exported goods worth R1.04 billion to the rest of Africa.[44] This figure excludes indirect exports, estimated at about R400 million.[45] Exports to the rest of Africa (outside the SACU) represented 5.5 percent of South Africa's total exports, and exports to BLS 5 percent.[46] There was a marked imbalance in the direction of trade, imports from the rest of Africa totaling only R317 million.

Since 1981, however, South Africa's exports to the rest of Africa have declined both in volume and value: food exports have been wiped out by drought, and African countries have faced increased foreign-exchange problems. Although South Africa is holding its share of the southern African market, it has no credit lines or special financing facilities available to enable it to expand its trade with the rest of the continent.[47]

The BLS countries are the most dependent of the SADCC states on trade with South Africa, which is also Zimbabwe's major trading partner, Zambia's second most important supplier, and the chief source of imports for Malawi and Mozambique.[48] The majority of Angola's trade with Africa in fact is with South Africa, and South African goods also find their way into Tanzania, albeit indirectly.

South Africa is the dominant source of manufactured goods for most of the nine countries; if this position is to be changed detailed planning and coordination will be required. It has been stated that the SADCC countries tend to produce a similar range of manufactured goods—leather, foodstuffs, textiles, handicrafts—and that therefore they do not need to trade with one another as they do not supply one another's needs. Complementary rather than competitive industries are needed if trade within the grouping is to be increased. However, a SADCC investigation into industrial and trade potential has found an unexpectedly large variation in national surplus capacity and shortages, and a number of industrial products with trade potential have been identified. SADCC believes that the distribution of industrial output among member countries could be coordinated, but there are few if any examples of such planning having worked satisfactorily anywhere.

Whereas the existence of competitive industries in countries forming a customs union is regarded as essential for trade creation within the union,[49] in a loose association such as SADCC a country can keep out competitive imports through tariff protection or quantitative restrictions. Zimbabwe recently has protected its clothing industry by restricting imports from Botswana.[50] SADCC's aim of encouraging intraregional trade may be difficult to accomplish in the case of competitive industries.

Zimbabwean industry depends heavily on exports to South Africa. It represents 7,000 jobs and R66 million per annum in foreign exchange. In 1980 Zimbabwean exports of manufactured goods to South Africa totaled R116 million, of which R70 million was covered by the trade agreement. If the trade agreement were terminated, these exports could not compete on the South African market.[51] According to Hill, "it seems likely that officials concerned with trade promotion will be promoting trade with South Africa as energetically as with other partners, despite the overall SADCC intention to move towards disengagement from South Africa, and it seems unlikely that Zimbabwe will be able to afford materially to change this relationship in the near future."[52]

Zimbabwe apparently can gain very little at present by switching its trade to the north. Although the demand is there, the currencies are weak. Many of these countries face severe shortages of hard currency; Zimbabwe, in fact, also has the same problem. Often it is South Africa that benefits from this shortage; if the problem is to be overcome, interregional payments need to be improved and some sort of barter system instituted. Attention is being given to the feasibility of eliminating foreign-exchange payments by setting up a system of balancing and clearing accounts (under the proposed development bank), which would operate not only for merchandise exports but also for transport services. However, this mechanism would work only if individual states would then give priority to purchasing from their debtors.

The fact that the currencies of the nine are not convertible is a major barrier to trade. Possible solutions being investigated are bartering (which is becoming increasingly important in Africa) and the use of local currencies along the lines of the Tanzania-Mozambique trade protocol.[53]

Preferential treatment is also required to boost trade within the bloc. For example, countries with import-licensing systems could give preference to fellow SADCC members, whereas those operating tariff systems could grant concessions. The problem here, however, relates to various other agreements in which SADCC states are parties. The SACU agreement does not allow the BLS countries to grant preferences to other countries, the PTA does not allow trade preferences to be given among the nine SADCC states that are not also extended to other PTA countries, and various agreements with the EEC through Lomé II might present further barriers.

Although there is certainly scope for increasing intra-SADCC trade, it is unlikely that some of the countries (especially BLS) will be able to obtain basic consumer goods as cheaply as from South Africa or that SADCC will be able to provide the range of manufactured goods that South Africa does. Established trade patterns also are difficult to break down; for example, a report quotes Zambia as preferring to trade with South Africa than with the rest of the continent: South African firms supply a wider variety of goods and pay promptly for imports, whereas other African countries ignore orders and are tardy in paying.[54] A considerable market for South Africa within SADCC seems assured for some time to come, although the composition of manufactured exports may change; as economic development proceeds in SADCC, its demand may shift to more sophisticated products in which South Africa would have a competitive edge.

Employment

In common with the rest of the Third World, SADCC states face the problem of creating sufficient employment opportunities to accommodate labor-market entrants. All the SADCC states have at one time or another exported labor to South Africa, and some continue to find South Africa an important—or at least useful—source of employment. Although manpower development and training is included in the SADCC Programme of Action, there is no formal program for the reduction of employment dependence on South Africa as there is, for example, in the spheres of transport and communications. Nevertheless, it is necessary to mention employment dependence in this chapter as the results of programs in other fields will affect the ability of individual countries to reduce this dependence.

Seven SADCC states (all, excluding Tanzania and Angola) agreed at a meeting in Gaborone in 1980 to form the Southern African Labour Commission (SALC) to harmonize and coordinate policies and practices with regard to the supply of migrant labor to South Africa. Tanzania was admitted as a member in 1983 at the same time that the SALC applied to become a subcommittee of SADCC.[55]

In 1982 the Zimbabwean government announced that no more local recruiting of labor for South African mines would be allowed, and in effect, only five SADCC states now supply labor to South Africa, principally to the mining industry. The trend is downward—for internal South African political and economic reasons quite apart from any actions by SADCC states to curb supplies. On the political side, legislative changes have resulted in residents of homelands receiving preference over foreign Africans in the job market, and this preference has been reinforced by the growing employment problem among Africans both inside and outside the homelands. Thus, within the structure of CONSAS, the independent homelands are exerting pressure on Pretoria to give preference to their residents in labor placement.

Paradoxically, therefore, attempts by SADCC countries to reduce their dependence on labor exports may be superfluous in the light of trends in the South African labor market. If these trends persist, the exporting countries obviously will have to try to absorb all of their own labor forces in due course.

The important question is whether these countries can afford to cut off supplies of labor and, if so, whether they can create sufficient jobs to absorb their own labor. The possibilities vary from country to country.

Of the SALC members, Lesotho is by far the most dependent on labor exports to South Africa. In 1980 about 150,000 Sotho were employed in South Africa, as against only 40,000 in the wage sector at home, the balance of the labor force being in agriculture and the small informal sector. During its Third Five-Year Plan period (1980–1981 through 1984–1985), the modern sector was "not likely to absorb more than 20 percent of the job seekers."[56] Since the absorptive capacity of the agricultural sector is also low, there appears to be no possibility of Lesotho voluntarily withdrawing labor from South Africa.

There is another aspect to Lesotho's employment dependency—namely, the importance to its economy of the earnings of migrant workers and especially of deferred pay and remittances from the Chamber of Mines. As the SADCC background paper states: "Termination of the system [of migrant labour], without compensatory financial transfers from other sources, would pauperise the great majority of Basotho households."[57]

In the circumstances, the suggestion that Lesotho should institute a phased withdrawal of labor over a fifteen-year period must be dismissed as totally unrealistic.[58] In fact, as I have pointed out, the best long-term solution for Lesotho is probably closer economic integration with South Africa, for "without the free movement of labour to South Africa implied in a common market, its large-scale rural development is all but impossible."[59]

Of the other supplier states, the problems of reabsorption are probably greatest in Botswana. In the remaining countries—Malawi, Mozambique, and Swaziland—it should be easier to terminate migrant labor flows to South Africa. The SADCC background paper probably is correct in concluding that in these three countries "the problem of reabsorption of migrants is manageable, albeit difficult and costly."[60] The South African labor market continues to fulfill a most useful role for them by reducing unemployment and providing foreign exchange.

There is an interesting contrast between the emphasis in the SADCC background paper and that in the International Labor Organization (ILO) collection. Whereas the latter recommends that the supplier states themselves initiate a phased program of withdrawal, the former stresses the problems that they would face if South Africa reduced the opportunities for migrants or terminated the system! The SADCC paper thus recommends a policy of maximizing benefits from the migrant labor system and preparing contingency plans to reduce the costs of a "sudden reduction or termination" of opportunities for migrant labor.[61] It stresses the need for an urgent study of employment possibilities in Lesotho.[62]

Although one of the stated aims of the SALC is ultimately to eliminate migrant labor, this seems to be an impossible one for Lesotho and a relatively remote one for the other four countries.

Dependence and Interdependence

Most economic relationships involve interdependence rather than only dependence. This section has dealt with the question of SADCC's dependence on South Africa, but what about the reverse?

In the field of transport, for instance, South African dependence on SADCC is found in the use of the harbor at Maputo and of neighboring rail and road systems to reach export markets. The rail link under construction with Swaziland involves potential interdependence, as it will provide the shortest and lowest-cost route to Richards Bay for several million tons per annum of mineral exports from the Transvaal lowveld. The South African Transport Services (SAT) conveys and handles a considerable volume of SADCC traffic but cannot be said to be dependent on this traffic, which provides less than 2 percent of its total revenues.[63]

So far as trade is concerned, not only do SADCC markets absorb almost one-tenth of South Africa's exports, but a calculation for 1979 showed that over 5 percent of value added and some 300,000 jobs in all sectors could be attributed to the level of exports to BLS alone.[64] These figures sound high but seem to illustrate that trade with SADCC is important to South Africa.

The Electricity Supply Commission (ESCOM) in South Africa is to receive a maximum of 8 percent of its supplies from the Cahora Bassa hydroelectricity scheme in Mozambique. An electricity grid and hence increased interdependence between South Africa and its neighbors is developing; at present Lesotho; Swaziland; and parts of Mozambique, Zimbabwe, and Botswana receive power from ESCOM.[65] Mozambique feeds into the ESCOM grid; the others have the potential to do so too, a good example being Lesotho, the proposed Highland Water Scheme of which is based on the sale of power to ESCOM and of water to the southern Transvaal industrial region.

South Africa, Swaziland, and Mozambique have a joint water agreement concluded in 1983, governing the common use of waters of five rivers. Mozambique, Zimbabwe, and Botswana have met in Maputo to consider the use of the waters of the Limpopo River, and it is hoped to establish a joint technical committee.[66]

The BLS countries and Zimbabwe traditionally have been dependent on South African investment—in mining, manufacturing, distribution, and tourism. Of these countries, it is BLS that would find it most difficult to replace South Africa: because of their membership in the SACU and/ or RMA, they are virtually extensions of the South African economy, and this means that much of their foreign investment is by South African firms or South African branches of overseas companies. Their small economic size (small populations and low per capita incomes) provides another reason that they have not attracted the interest of overseas investors to any significant extent. In contrast, Zimbabwe has a far larger, more diversified economy with good growth potential if politicoeconomic conditions are favorable. In that case Zimbabwe may have considerable attraction for investors from abroad, particularly since it is the most developed of the SADCC countries.

The tourist industry in these three countries, as well as in Zimbabwe and Malawi, is dominated by South African visitors. South Africans as a proportion of total visitors are roughly 90 percent for Lesotho, 60–65 percent for Swaziland, and 36 percent for Zimbabwe, as well as 15 percent for Malawi.[67] There is considerable South African investment in hotels in the BLS countries; and, with one exception, all casinos in these states are controlled by a South African group, albeit with a substantial local (government or parastatal) shareholding. South Africa also was the major source of tourists in preindependence Mozambique.

An important aspect of interdependence is symmetry. A useful approach to analyzing this question in the case of SADCC is to employ the concepts of *sensitivity* and *vulnerability* dependence.[68] Sensitivity refers to the degree of responsiveness within a given (unchanged) policy framework: How quickly and at what cost do changes in one country cause changes in another? Vulnerability refers to the ability of a country to adjust to changing circumstances over a period of time. Based on the previous discussions in this chapter, the types of dependence may be assessed as in table 6–2.

This table illustrates that high-vulnerability dependence is exhibited in a number of sectors by Lesotho (because of a poor resource base and geographical position), in tourism by the BLS countries, and in some sectors by South Africa. Some qualifications are necessary, however. Although tourism is important in the BLS economies, it is possible that they may be able to adjust over time to having a diminished tourist industry, but probably not without some difficulty. South Africa's vul-

Table 6–2
Types of Dependence in SADCC–South African Relations

Sector	Sensitivity	Vulnerability
Rail/road	Botswana, Lesotho, Malawi, Mozambique, Swaziland, South Africa, Zambia, Zimbabwe	Lesotho (South Africa?)
Ports	Botswana, Lesotho, Malawi, Mozambique, South Africa, Zambia, Zimbabwe	Lesotho
Airports	Botswana, Lesotho, Swaziland	
Trade	*Imports:* Botswana, Lesotho, Malawi, Mozambique, Swaziland, Zambia, Zimbabwe	Lesotho
	Exports: Lesotho, South Africa, Zimbabwe	Lesotho (South Africa?)
Employment	Botswana, Lesotho, Malawi, Mozambique, South Africa, Swaziland	Lesotho (South Africa?)
Fuel	Botswana, Lesotho, Swaziland, Zimbabwe	Lesotho
Coal	Lesotho	Lesotho
Tourism	Botswana, Lesotho, Malawi, Swaziland, Zimbabwe	Botswana, Lesotho, Swaziland

nerability, however, is qualified according to its ability to find alternative export markets and hence the necessity to use neighboring railway systems. In the field of employment South Africa may not find it so easy entirely to replace Sotho mine labor. The conclusion, nevertheless, must be that there is an asymmetry in the relationship in Pretoria's favor. The extent of SADCC dependence on South Africa in the fields of transport, trade, and employment is likely to be substantial for some years to come; but the potential undoubtedly exists for an overall reduction of links. However, this potential varies from country to country, and the costs of adjustment might be substantial.

Table 6–2 excludes the water and power sectors. As the downstream countries, Swaziland and Mozambique could be both highly sensitive and highly vulnerable to South African actions; in the same way, Lesotho and Swaziland could be highly sensitive in the field of electricity. The proposed Highland Water Scheme in Lesotho could introduce a high degree of sensitivity and vulnerability into water and power relations between that country and South Africa, and it is a moot point which of the two would be in the more dependent position. Exports of water and power could become Lesotho's main source of revenue, but merely by agreeing to the project Pretoria would in fact concede a considerable measure of its present self-sufficiency. Perhaps the issue could be settled by locating the main power plant in South Africa, as apparently has been considered in an earlier feasibility study; this would ensure an allocation of key installations to both countries.

Although the aim of SADCC is one of reducing economic dependence on South Africa, it must be noted that this aim has been questioned from four different perspectives.[69]

1. Skeptics doubt whether member governments have either the wish or the will to accept the economic sacrifices implied.
2. Some critics argue that disengagement would neither harm South Africa seriously nor save the SADCC countries from racist retribution—that is, military retaliation.
3. Another view is that a preoccupation with economic disengagement may lead to an abandonment of the commitment to political liberation.
4. Radicals believe that the approach of concentrating on South Africa as the primary target is misconceived: The major problem is international capitalism, not South African economic dominance of the region.

The second and third points lead to a consideration of future political relationships between SADCC and Pretoria.

The Future: In the Wake of Nkomati

The future of SADCC would appear to depend largely on political developments in the subcontinent, and specifically on those involving South
Africa. As the major economic and military power in the region, South
Africa has shown that it has the means to destabilize neighboring countries, at least in the short term. Although in 1984 there was a flurry of
diplomatic action between Pretoria and its neighbors, destabilization still
remained a policy of last resort. A review of the state of SADCC–South
African relations, therefore, is necessary.

SADCC Attitudes

SADCC has adopted a pragmatic and realistic attitude toward Pretoria.
Its documents consistently reiterate that links with South Africa will have
to be maintained for a long time to come and that, in fact, trade might
increase in the short term. The aim is one of gradual disengagement from
South Africa—that is, essentially over the long term. SADCC also has
acknowledged that it has a stake in preventing the imposition of mandatory sanctions against South Africa. This has been publicly acknowledged by the leaders of all those countries bordering South Africa. In
1984, however, statements issued after SADCC meetings have been interpreted as signifying a move toward increasing militancy,[70] but although South Africa's destabilizing role was criticized in the final
communiqué issued after the Maseru and Lusaka meetings, in 1983 and
1984 respectively, the latter acknowledged that there were signs of a less
aggressive stance on the part of Pretoria.[71]

There apparently have been clear differences in response among
SADCC states to the problems of relationships with South Africa. Reducing dependence on Pretoria is only one of SADCC's objectives, and
not all member states regard this as the pivotal issue.[72]

So far as SADCC policies are concerned, its Programme of Action is
a realistic one. Cognizance has been taken of the position of the BLS
countries and their long-standing economic relationships with South Africa. Joint projects with South Africa, such as the Swaziland-Komati-
poort and Botswana-Ellisras rail links, and the Highland Water Scheme
in Lesotho, have met with SADCC approval despite being in apparent
conflict with the objective of reducing dependence. The view within
SADCC is that these projects are economically important to BLS and
that, by strengthening their economies, they will enable these countries
ultimately to become more independent of South Africa.

South African Attitudes

Pretoria's policy toward SADCC has been the subject of much attention, analysts tending to agree with Vale's identification of two distinct groups—namely, *hawks* and *doves*.[73] Briefly, the argument is that the hawks believe that its economic and military power are Pretoria's only available instruments to ensure its security in the face of what they perceive as a commitment by neighboring countries to destabilize South Africa through support for the ANC. Pretoria therefore should retaliate by manipulating economic ties and supporting disaffected groups in these countries, thereby keeping them economically dependent and militarily weak. The doves, in contrast, believe that such an aggressive stance would alienate the West and generally harm the country's international relations. They consequently favor the strengthening of economic ties so as to induce the SADCC states to adopt a reasonable approach.

The military issue is discussed later in this chapter. Examples of the manipulation of economic ties that frequently are quoted are the threatened termination of the preferential-trade agreement with Zimbabwe; the repatriation of migrant labor to Zimbabwe; delays in the transportation of key imports, such as foodstuffs and petroleum; and the withdrawal of locomotives and wagons on loan from South Africa to Zimbabwe. Such actions certainly were not taken at the instigation of the SAT, which has long-standing and amicable working agreements with railway organizations in the subcontinent. Indeed, the then general manager of the SAT, Dr. J.G.H. Loubser—a strong advocate of so-called transport diplomacy—and his successor reiterated their willingness to help neighboring states overcome their transport problems. At any one time, there are at least 7,000 SAT wagons on foreign rail systems and more than 1,500 foreign wagons on the SAT network. South African wagons are hauled as far as Zaire and occasionally even into Tanzania. The SAT has always been willing to assist; for example, it has seconded management and engineering staff to Malawi and Swaziland and has assisted in clearing blockages caused by derailments and accidents on the Komatipoort-Maputo line.[74]

It is true that the SAT has withheld shipments on occasion, but only to induce the return of wagons. The South African government, however, has intervened in normal working relationships between railway administrations by insisting on discussions at the ministerial level.[75] This level has been unacceptable to Zimbabwe; and, ultimately, talks have been held at a senior-official level.

It has been argued that it was in the formulation of policy toward Zimbabwe that the different strands of South African thought were polarized, and that the hardliners—those who believe that "the gun and the maize train will speak louder than a hundred speeches at the United Nations"[76]—came to the fore. In public statements, however, South African government spokesmen have come across as doves favoring peaceful relations with prosperous and stable neighbors.[77] Government spokesmen and academics have also mentioned the importance of economic development in neighboring countries and of a positive view toward such development.

The economic approach is the one that is favored by the private sector, which realizes the importance of the SADCC market. Public statements from both business and government during the last few years represent a considerable improvement on earlier South African attitudes. The unfortunate appellation *counterconstellation* probably led to an initial antagonism toward SADCC, but the fact that the formation of the grouping was greeted with considerable skepticism—by politicians, businessmen, and the press—probably reflected the conventional wisdom in South Africa—that its inclusion is a sine qua non for a subcontinental economic grouping to succeed. The automatic assumption is that South African economic growth would spill over its borders and that, because of the strength of trade, transport, and other ties, closer economic relationships (often referred to as a common market) with Pretoria are both necessary and desirable for the optimal development of its neighbors. This assumption, however, is theoretically unsound (as illustrated earlier) and conflicts with empirical evidence on the relationship between *core* and *periphery*.

From an economist's point of view, there is no good reason that South Africa should be unduly sensitive about the aims of SADCC; they are natural, given one large, dominant country in a region. There are a number of analogies—for example, Canada and Mexico versus the United States and West African states versus Nigeria. In fact, there are good reasons that development in neighboring states should be welcomed. South Africa's priority is to develop its own poorer regions, and it does not have the resources—financial, manpower, or infrastructural—to devote to the economic development of the subcontinent. It is itself only a middle-income country and therefore should welcome an infusion of foreign aid to SADCC, particularly as it is clear that trade and other ties will be maintained for many years.

Pre-Nkomati: Destabilization

What politicians say is one thing; what actually happens in practice is another. If pragmatism has tended to prevail at the economic and operational level in SADCC–South African relations, the position has been murky in the politicomilitary arena in the pre-Nkomati period. It has been widely held that Pretoria as well as certain neighbors (in their individual or frontline capacity, not under the SADCC umbrella) have aided and abetted insurgents. These charges have been denied by both sides, but clearly a climate in which neighboring countries provide bases for armed infiltration into South Africa, and South Africa in turn retaliates either by direct military action or by assisting guerrillas, not only would disrupt progress (for example, by damaging the transport network in Mozambique) but also would lead to unnecessarily strained political relations.

A problem facing South African commentators is that legislation makes it difficult, if not impossible, to acquire official information on military operations. They thus operate under a disadvantage perhaps not always appreciated by their foreign counterparts, and must rely on foreign sources or local leaks for their information. Although the media in South Africa gave much publicity to the country's military incursions into Angola and raids on Maputo and Maseru, and there was no doubt where Pretoria's sympathies lay in the internal politics of Angola, Mozambique, and Zimbabwe, its position with regard to Lesotho—the fourth target of alleged destabilization—remained ambiguous. Foreign sources, however, have had little doubt about South African support for the MNR in Mozambique, UNITA in Angola, and the Lesotho Liberation Army. However, the credentials of the MNR and UNITA as political movements in countries where the will of the population never has been tested in elections often are overlooked.[78]

South Africa—through its overt raids into Angola, Maputo, and Maseru, and its perceived support for insurgents in neighboring countries—had gained the reputation of "a regional ruffian or desperado."[79] A continuation of such policies could have proved costly; it was becoming more and more likely that that SADCC donor countries would take an increasingly hard line against Pretoria wherever projects that they had funded were the targets of destabilization. A particularly tough line was taken at Maseru by Edgard Pisani, the commissioner of the EEC, who referred to the destruction of EEC projects. Although not confident about the possibility of imposing sanctions, he did not rule out the fact that the growing tide of public opinion in the EEC could lead to the implementation of a policy of disinvestment in South Africa. Pretoria, in turn, believed that it was the object of a concerted attempt at destabilization by African states demanding a change both in the behavior of the government—that is, in its race policies—and in its structure—that is, replacing a minority (white) with a majority (black) government.[80] This perception on the part of Pretoria may be wrong. Anglin writes: "A peaceful resolution of the conflict would be the most attractive outcome for a majority, if not all the Frontline States. Since 1969 they have been committed, under the Lusaka Manifesto, to just such a settlement. Moreover, they would probably be prepared to accept something short of full majority rule, at least initially, provided a formula for meaningful power-sharing could be devised."[81]

The position toward the end of 1983 was that the South African prime minister had invited African countries to sign nonaggression pacts and treaties prohibiting aid or sanctuary to insurgents, whereas the secretary-general of SADCC had appealed to South Africa to join in creating peace in the subcontinent. The words were there from both sides, but the will to translate them into practice was not apparent, despite ministerial meetings between South Africa and Angola in the Cape Verde Islands (in December 1982 and February 1983) and the disclosure—during the visit of Roelof F. Botha, the South African foreign minister, to Lisbon at the end of November 1983—that discussions between his country and Mozambique had been held in Komatipoort in December 1982 and May 1983. (This visit by Botha appears to have been connected with that by President Samora Machel of Mozambique to Portugal and other Western countries.) It was apparent, however, that there were two clear options open to southern African countries. The first was to eschew giving aid or refuge to dissident groups. This would remove the basis for aggression. Presumably resources would then be devoted to meeting the economic goals of SADCC and CONSAS. Alternatively, aid and refuge could continue to be given, resulting in continued aggression. Economic progress by both sides would be retarded, and the danger of conflict would increase.

The Nkomati Accord

Events moved rapidly following the return of the foreign minister to Pretoria. By Christmas 1983 delegations from South Africa and Mozambique had met in Swaziland to discuss certain aspects of mutual cooperation, and early in the New Year a joint communiqué on these talks was issued stating that four joint working groups would meet in mid-January in Pretoria and Maputo. These groups were concerned with security, economic affairs, the Cahora Bassa project, and tourism.

The work of these groups culminated in the Nkomati Accord, which was signed by the president of Mozambique and the prime minister of South Africa in March 1984. It is essentially a nonaggression treaty committing the countries to the principles of good neighborliness and the peaceful coexistence of different political and economic systems. In his speech, the president stated that he rejected any relationship that would increase economic dependence and reaffirmed his country's total adherence to the principles of SADCC's Lusaka Declaration; SADCC was not anti–South African but refused to be economically dependent on South Africa. The prime minister, again referring to a constellation of states, tended to emphasize the economic advantages of southern African countries working together.[82]

Although negotiations between South Africa and Mozambique had been comprehensive, there was also the complementary Lusaka Agreement between South Africa and Angola on troop withdrawals. This agreement was concluded in February 1984 at discussions that were also attended by the United States. A Joint Monitoring Commission (JMC) was established and commenced work at the beginning of March to observe the orderly withdrawal of South African troops from Angola. This move implies the cessation of Pretoria's support for UNITA and was tied to the vexed question of Namibian independence.

Post-Nkomati: Rapprochement?

Other SADCC countries were represented at the signing of the Nkomati Accord by their ambassadors to Maputo. The accord (and the Lusaka Agreement) drew mixed reactions from various quarters.

The leaders of the six frontline states, which include Angola and Mozambique, met in Arusha at the end of April. Although approving of the agreements, the communiqué was careful to add that apartheid was the root cause of South Africa's problems and that their objective was to eliminate it by whatever means, preferably peaceful.[83] They appealed for foreign aid to consolidate their fragile economies; this was important if they were to be able to play a constructive role in the search for peace and freedom in the subcontinent. They expressed the hope that South Africa would honor its commitments.[84]

Of the remaining SADCC countries, Malawi expressed a special interest in the success of the accord. Its minister of transport and communications stated that Malawi looked forward to reaping the benefits of the accord as 70 percent of its exports normally used the port of Beira.[85]

A number of other SADCC countries also held discussions with South Africa in the immediate post-Nkomati period. The BLS countries have regular customs union and/or monetary meetings with Pretoria, and Malawi has diplomatic relations; but what is different about recent negotiations is that they revolved around the security issue.

In 1984 the South African and Swaziland governments announced that they had in fact concluded a security agreement in 1983, and agreed to exchange trade representatives and establish trade missions. On his return home, the Swazi prime minister was quoted as saying that "our

main aim was to *strengthen* the already strong ties with South Africa"[86]—
a contradiction of the SADCC aim of reducing links.

Delegations from Botswana visited South Africa for talks on security
matters. The South African foreign minister made it clear that they were
not negotiating an accord but, rather, practical arrangements to prevent
violence being planned in either country.[87] Concurrently the president of
Botswana, speaking in Washington,[88] stated that his country was under
pressure from Pretoria to sign an accord but that, since there were no
hostilities, a nonaggression pact was unnecessary. According to him, South
Africa had threatened to deploy its troops along the border and to make
conditions more difficult at the border posts through which most of
Botswana's foreign trade passes. However, Botswana would not sign a
pact as this would mean giving up its independence and making a major
shift in its foreign policy.

South Africa and Lesotho met on a number of occasions in 1984. It
was reported that South Africa wanted a nonaggression pact and that,
failing to obtain one, that the Highland Water Scheme and continued
acceptance of Sotho migrant labor would be threatened.[89] Lesotho provides an example of the limits of the Nkomati approach: Despite its
being the country most dependent on South Africa, threats have not
worked to date; it has resisted signing a pact; and the water-project study
is going ahead.

In 1984 South Africa's foreign minister visited Malawi, and it was
reported that there were strong indications that he had been to a number
of other African countries, that the prime minister had met various African leaders, and that a large number of cabinet ministers from African
countries had visited South Africa.[90]

The most significant deliberations, however, almost certainly were
those on the Namibian issue, bringing together SWAPO and the Multi-
Party Conference (MPC). Although no substantial progress was made at
the talks, two important developments were Pretoria's agreeing to independence provided the MPC and SWAPO could agree, and SWAPO's
empowering its leader to sign a cease-fire agreement with South Africa.
As against these points, however, the MPC insisted that the UN should
recognize the internal parties and withdraw its recognition of SWAPO
as the sole representative of the Namibian people. The question of Cuban
withdrawal from Angola remained unsolved. A parallel resolution of the
Angolan conflict and Namibian independence will be required.

Implementing the Accord

Since the signing of the Nkomati Accord there has been considerable
activity on the part of both governments to implement the terms and to
ensure that the gains each party expects will be forthcoming.

Mozambique's Gains. The economy of Mozambique has taken a considerable battering since independence. The result was that, in 1984 and 1985, its economy was in a precarious position and there was a serious shortage of most commodities. A report of the National Planning Commission calculated that Mozambique had lost R7 billion since independence, of which R4.75 billion was estimated to be due to South African activities (including a fall in the number of migrant laborers recruited, the abandonment of the system whereby the salaries of mine workers were paid in gold at a preferential price, a decline in traffic through Maputo and the consequent loss of railway and harbor revenue, and support for the MNR).[91] No mention was made of the cessation of tourism—an activity not encouraged since independence—but its effect on the economy must have been considerable.

Clearly, Mozambique hoped that the accord, by leading to greater security, would pave the way for foreign investment and encourage the resumption of traditional trade routes serving the Transvaal as well as Zimbabwe, Zambia, and Malawi. Its envisaged gains, therefore, were political (the military defeat and hence political demise of the MNR) and economic. The sheer security requirements of the Machel government are not replicated elsewhere in southern Africa except in Angola, and economic links between Mozambique and South Africa have endured; both were important factors behind the accord.

South Africa's Gains. Similarly, South Africa expects both political and economic gains from the accord as well as from its agreement with Angola, any other nonaggression pacts it may conclude with neighbors, and Namibian independence. Not only has defense claimed a large share of the budget for a considerable period, but it is felt in government circles that, even when returns to South African private investment in Namibia are taken into account, the cost of public administration in the territory represents a net drain on the economy (the prime minister made much of this point during his European tour in mid-1984). These defense and administrative costs thus could better be channeled into pressing domestic areas such as housing and education.

Politically, South Africa expects gains on three fronts. In regional terms it anticipates a recognition that problems should be solved by countries in the region rather than by intervention from abroad. Its mixture of military, economic, and diplomatic pressure on its neighbors has paid off, and the peacemakers can now replace the hawks. The virtual isolation of the ANC means that, in effect, a new cordon sanitaire has been established.

Internally, the reduced threat of ANC guerrilla infiltration is expected to give Pretoria time to concentrate on the implementation of the new constitution, black housing and education, and related issues. Internationally, South Africa hoped for credit for its actions and a reduction in its isolation.

Can the Parties Deliver? An important, perhaps crucial, question following from the Nkomati Accord is whether South Africa and Mozambique can satisfy each other's expectations. For the government of Mozambique, the main issues relate to security, efficiency of public administration, and the creation of a climate favorable for foreign investment.

Security. As noted previously, it has not been easy to overcome the MNR. There has been speculation that South Africa may be obliged to assist the Mozambiquan forces.

Administrative Efficiency. An improvement in managerial and technical efficiency in public administration is of fundamental importance, particularly in the transport sector, which is a key to increased revenue earning for Mozambique. It is anticipated that expatriate skills will be obtained, and South Africa and Britain already are lending a hand.

Investment Climate. An improved security situation, coupled with greater administrative efficiency, would provide a more attractive proposition for foreign investment and tourism. But a moderation of some of the economic policies of government also seems to be important, and there is an awareness of this fact: Machel has pointed out that poor management of state companies and wage increases unaccompanied by increases in output are contributory factors to the country's poor economic performance.[92] The government announced in 1980 that it would denationalize certain operations, and in 1985 was examining legislation to encourage an expanded private sector and foreign investment. It is also negotiating membership in the World Bank and the International Monetary Fund, and this will provide access to drawing rights and technical expertise. However, it will take a while yet to restore the confidence of businessmen. This is an extremely important point, as there may be a danger of too great an expectation on the part of Mozambique regarding foreign investment. Two views in South African business circles may be distinguishable: (1) that it would be foolish to invest until the climate has improved, and (2) that investment now is a necessary risk if the potential benefits of the accord are to be realized.

South Africa's contribution to the accord will have to be focused on the Cahora Bassa project, security, transport, tourism, and industrial and commercial investment. It is doubtful, for the reasons outlined earlier, that South Africa can increase its intake of migrant labor from neighboring countries, although it could perhaps use the accord as a lever against Lesotho by granting preference to recruits from Mozambique.

Cahora Bassa. As mentioned earlier, there is an agreement covering the supply of electricity from the Cahora Bassa dam; two power lines supplying South Africa came into service in 1979, but the scheme never operated to its maximum and in fact was completed only recently on the strength of a R50 million credit granted by South Africa to Portugal. Interest on the loan is being paid by Portugal, which can be refunded by Mozambique only when output is resumed.

Security. This agreement also provides for South Africa and Mozambique to take steps to protect the transmission lines, and the Joint Security Commission established in terms of the Nkomati Accord is handling the operation. It could include the use of South African air and ground forces to patrol the lines.

Transport. Maputo remains the natural port for the southern Transvaal industrial region—South Africa's major urban and manufacturing region—as well as for the Transvaal lowveld. Transport officials have visited Johannesburg to canvass business for the port, and the director of the Mozambiquan Railways has stated that Maputo is "useless' without South African trade.[93] Transvaal coal and steel, however, have moved to Richards Bay in recent years and appear unlikely to revert to Maputo, at least until they can be assured of a similar level of efficiency. It is possible, however, that EEC countries importing South African coal may insist on the use of Maputo as a form of aid. As mentioned earlier, the SAT has played an important role from time to time in the management of the port, and the private sector could assist further in this regard.

Tourism. Some 107,500 South Africans visited Mozambique annually before independence. Clearly, South Africa is the major market, and a Mozambiquan delegation visited South Africa in 1984 to discuss tourist promotion and visas. Hotels are being refurbished, and a leading South African hotel chain is reported to be interested in investing in Mozambique. But it will take a considerable effort to restore the industry to its previous level in view of changes in the patterns of tourism in the subcontinent in the last ten years.

Investment. Prior to independence in 1975 much of the industrial investment in Mozambique was attributable to South African firms and

South African subsidiaries of multinational corporations. Some of these companies have continued operating, albeit at well below full capacity, but many have closed down. They may now consider reactivating their dormant plants. A South African government mission visited Maputo in 1984 for talks on the channeling of investment inquiries to the Mozambiquan government. However, organized industry in South Africa believes that private investors will need government guarantees and lines of credit.[94]

An important point is that the Accord has been signed at a low point in the South African business cycle. The economy has been hard hit by the sluggish world economy, the low gold price, and drought; and the government has commitments to the new constitution, homeland development, urban housing, African education, and transport. It is not in a position, therefore, to offer much in the way of financial aid to Mozambique. A key role will have to be played by the West, not only in providing public and private investment funds but also in demonstrating that the market-economy system is superior to central planning.

Effect of Nkomati on SADCC

The Nkomati Accord has been interpreted as having implications for SADCC's goal of regional economic self-sufficiency and reducing dependence on South Africa. The validity of this contention can be judged only by relating it to the main fields of SADCC–South Africa contact—namely, transport, trade, and employment.

The maritime countries hold the key to reducing SADCC's perceived dependence on South Africa. In this respect the port and rail systems of Mozambique are of crucial importance. If the Nkomati Accord leads to stability in Mozambique, and if it is accompanied by increased efficiency in the transport sector, then normal SADCC trade routes could be resumed. Far from militating against SADCC's goals, therefore, the Accord probably would further them: The use of the South African transport network would decline, and alternative trading patterns might be facilitated. The impetus given to economic growth in Mozambique could enable it to reduce its dependence on employment in South Africa for its labor force, particularly if its largely untapped mineral and other resources were to be developed. Mozambique's dependence on South Africa might be increased in aspects such as tourism and the port of Maputo (the latter a case of interdependence anyway), but for SADCC as a whole it cannot be said that the accord is a contradiction. The same would not necessarily hold true, of course, for similar agreements between South Africa and other SADCC states.

Conclusion

Despite both the enormity of the task faced by SADCC in meeting its goals, and unsettled political conditions in the subcontinent, most foreign observers appear cautiously optimistic about the grouping's future. Major aid donors, firms involved in SADCC projects, and diplomats were optimistic at the Maseru meeting in 1983, after which it was stated that SADCC's program had "gathered renewed although still modest pace."[95] The Canadian International Development Agency was sufficiently impressed after the Lusaka meeting to state that SADCC would be a priority in its future African lending.[96]

Some skepticism still prevails, however. One journal pointed out that "for all its good intentions SADCC is riven with contradictions,"[97] and that, for the BLS countries, which it regards as having little realistic chance of breaking free from South African economic links, "SADCC's wider separationist aims are simply pie in the sky."[98] *The Economist* has been consistently skeptical of the organization's ability to reduce the economic dependence of its members on South Africa.[99]

Discussions with government officials and businessmen in some SADCC countries reveal that, in general, although the idea is considered a good one and it is hoped that it will succeed, there is considerable doubt as to its chances. There are signs that not all member countries may yet be convinced of the benefits of SADCC membership, at least in the short term. Thus the chairman of the National Industrial Development Corporation of Swaziland has stated that the real benefits of SADCC probably were long term and yet to be seen, and those of the SACU were immediate.[100] Similarly, the then acting head of the Swaziland Central Statistical Office stated that SADCC was still a young organization and Swaziland did not know whether or not it would benefit; SADCC was too big and too diverse, and he did not see how diverse ideologies could be harmonized. Also, SADCC could not replace the SACU insofar as Swaziland's revenue earning was concerned.[101]

The last point seems irrelevant as membership in the SACU is entirely compatible with that in SADCC. In fact, Swaziland's (and Lesotho's) overlapping membership in the four groupings—SACU, RMA, SADCC, and PTA—could well act as a spur to industrialization: Products manufactured there would have duty-free access to the markets of the SACU and preferential access to those of the PTA, and marketing would be facilitated by any transport and communications improvements under

SADCC. These two countries, together with Botswana, in theory could prove an attractive location for South African industrialists looking for access to such markets as well as for overseas companies wishing to exploit the customs union market without experiencing the political pressures often associated with investing in South Africa. It remains to be seen, however, whether the advent of the PTA and SADCC will make any significant difference to industrial investment in BLS; so far, overseas firms have continued to locate in South Africa while South African products continue to find their way into African markets.

Despite some reservations, however, there is no sign of any country wishing to withdraw from SADCC. On the contrary, a number of countries (including Zaire) apparently have expressed an interest in joining, but SADCC believes it should consolidate its structure further before expanding.[102]

How justified is optimism or pessimism about SADCC? The organization's achievements thus far appear to be that it has (1) established a structure for cooperation and regular meetings in a number of spheres, (2) embarked on a realistic program of projects concerning infrastructure and agriculture, and (3) brought the needs of the region to the attention of donors.

It certainly is unrealistic to expect to see the results of SADCC's efforts at this early stage of its history. Projects have a long gestation period. SADCC has been in existence for just five years, and many of its projects are now only at the negotiation stage; the majority will not be in operation until the second half of the 1980s. One cannot expect to see results, let alone miracles, overnight. But among the early projects to be completed are those in the telecommunications sector, which will overcome an important bottleneck for importers and exporters in the landlocked countries.

SADCC's potential appears to lie in the spheres of infrastructure (transport and communications) and production (of foodstuffs and energy) rather than in industry and trade. Its theoretical justification, on which to a great extent it ultimately must stand, is that it is a loose grouping rather than a form of economic integration. Despite this fact, however, the experience of attempts at the allocation of industries in economic groupings elsewhere in the world indicates that industrial cooperation is fraught with political problems—namely, the pull between national and regional goals. And its theoretical strength will be vitiated by any attempt to translate SADCC into "a kind of common market,"[103] as has been suggested. Not only is the potential complementarity of industrial structure required for intraregional trade lacking, but the problem of industrial polarization would occur.

SADCC may, however, be able to play an important role in stimulating trade between its members and the rest of the world. For example, it recently was reported that SADCC and the so-called like-minded countries (Australia, Austria, Belgium, Canada, Denmark, Finland, France, Ireland, Italy, The Netherlands, Norway, and Sweden) might join together in a mini-experiment along the lines of the proposed New International Economic Order (NIEO).[104] It is along these lines rather than the promotion of intra-SADCC trade that the grouping might find its best results; this is not to say that no attempt should be made to encourage intraregional trade, and the guidelines already laid down for trade mechanisms and payments arrangements (especially on reducing the use of scarce foreign exchange) are a step in the right direction.[105]

SADCC already has been most successful in focusing the attention, once a year, of major aid donors on southern Africa, and the importance of this function cannot be overlooked. All factors (political, military, or otherwise) affecting economic development in southern Africa are brought into focus at these meetings. SADCC probably is instrumental in changing the perceptions of donors about the subcontinent—something that may well be reflected in changing foreign policies in due course. SADCC also more effectively articulates the development needs of its members than does the OAU, Lomé, or any such body.

With regard to SADCC's future relations with Pretoria, it must be reemphasized that the long-term absorption of an apartheid-free South Africa would be theoretically justified only as long as no form of economic integration were contemplated; otherwise, South African industrial and trade domination in the region almost certainly would be accentuated. Even when the political issues in southern Africa have been resolved, however, and even if no economic integration is attempted, it is likely that one might expect a grouping such as SADCC to exist in order to counter South African economic hegemony. The existence of SADCC side by side with South Africa would not be an obstacle to regional economic *cooperation,* which is a different matter altogether from regional economic *integration.* In the meantime, agreements such as the Nkomati Accord between individual SADCC states and South Africa do not necessarily conflict with the organization's goal of reducing dependence on the subcontinent's dominant power. Moreover, it is at least as plausible an argument that, through political engagement with South Africa, SADCC countries may well be able to prod Pretoria more rapidly along the road to internal reform than they would be if they continued in their efforts to isolate the country politically.

The idea of SADCC as a loose grouping of countries working together cooperatively on a realistic program of action is theoretically justified. In practice, the pace of its progress is likely to be modest rather than spectacular, the key variables being the achievement of managerial and technical efficiency, the adoption of economic policies favorable to private foreign investment, and the eradication of the guerrilla factor. Despite the Nkomati Accord and other recent initiatives, open conflict remains the danger. It could severely dislocate moves toward greater economic cooperation in southern Africa.

Notes

1. These moves are sketched in the "Introduction" by the late Sir Seretse Khama to Amon J. Nsekela (ed.), *Southern Africa: Toward Economic Liberation* (London 1981). See also Gwendolen Carter, "Conflicting Aims in Southern Africa," Indiana University, 1982 (mimeo), 2. Despite the clear exposition of SADCC's founding in Nsekela, radical critics have identified an alternative explanation—namely, diplomatic initiatives of African and Western countries for a Marshall Plan type of reconstruction in postliberation southern Africa, to be financed by the West, especially the United States. See Roger Leys and Arno Tostensen, "Regional Co-operation in Southern Africa: The Southern African Development Co-ordination Conference," *Review of African Political Economy* XXIII (1982), 52. SADCC often is incorrectly referred to as the Southern African Development Co-ordination *Council*. In speech, the organization usually is referred to as "Sadec" rather than by the initials of the acronym SADCC.

2. For more detail on some of these points, see Richard F. Weisfelder, "The Southern African Development Coordination Conference (SADCC)," *South Africa International* XIII (1982), 80–84.

3. See, for example, William G. Demas, *The Economics of Development in Small Countries* (Montreal, 1965).

4. This section is based on Gavin G. Maasdorp, "New Economic Groupings in Southern Africa: PTA and SADCC," *Alternative Structures for Southern African Interaction* (Pretoria, 1982), 62.

5. Agence France Press (Paris), 26 July 1983.

6. Weisfelder, "SADCC," 81, also makes this point.

7. A.M. El-Agraa and A.J. Jones, *Theory of Customs Unions* (Oxford, 1981).

8. Peter Robson, *The Economics of International Integration* (London, 1980), 147.

9. Reginald H. Green, "Economic Co-ordination, Liberation and Development: Botswana-Namibia Perspectives" in Charles Harvey (ed.), *Papers on the Economy of Botswana* (London, 1981), 180.

10. SADCC, Blantyre Meeting Report, 1981, 11.

11. Ibid., 12.

12. Weisfelder, "SADCC," 80.

13. Ibid., 89; Carol B. Thompson, "SADCC: Toward the Economic Liberation of Southern Africa," paper presented at the African Studies Association meeting (1981), 40.

14. Weisfelder, "SADCC," 90.

15. *Times of Swaziland* (14 October 1982). See also *Daily News* (Durban), 9 April 1984; Norman MacQueen, "Mozambique's Widening Foreign Policy," *The World Today*, 40 (1984), 22–28.

16. Sometimes referred to as Renamo—in Portuguese the full name is Resistençia Naçional Moçambicana.

17. *African Business* (London), (December, 1983), describes prevailing conditions with regard to commodity shortages in Mozambique.

18. *Sunday Tribune* (Durban), 18 March 1984.

19. *African Economic Digest* (London), 4 February 1983.

20. Agence France Press, 29 March 1983.

21. Douglas G. Anglin, "SADCC versus PTA: Competitive or Complementary Approaches to Economic Liberation and Regional Cooperation in Southern Africa," paper presented at a meeting of the African Studies Association (1982).

22. Weisfelder, "SADCC," 88.

23. Although ibid., 17; Carter, "Aims," 16, differ somewhat in their descriptions of the process, they seem to agree on the effect of the division of sectoral responsibilities.

24. *African Report* (London) (May–June 1983); Agence France Press, 29 January 1983.

25. *African Business,* October 1983.

26. *Sunday Tribune,* 4 March 1984.

27. Ibid., 16. See also Christopher Hill, "Regional Cooperation in Southern Africa," *African Affairs* LXXXII (1983), 215–239.

28. Anglin, "SADCC," 37.

29. *The Herald* (Harare), 4 August 1982, confirming ibid., 41.

30. Weisfelder, "SADCC," 82.

31. F.A. Blumeris, "Statement to the Zimbabwe National Chamber of Commerce," Victoria Falls (19 May 1983), 18.

32. *Sunday Tribune,* 12 December 1982.

33. *The Herald,* 2 September 1983.

34. *African Business,* December 1982.

35. Ibid., January 1983.

36. Ibid., October 1983.

37. Weisfelder, "SADCC," 86.

38. *Africa Economic Digest,* 27 November 1981.

39. Information supplied to the author by a South African transport-company official.

40. *Africa Now* (London), December 1981.

41. Southern African Transport and Communications Commission, *Transport and Communications: Progress and Status* (Blantyre, 1981), II–51, II–52.

42. *Swazi Observer,* 7 May 1984.

43. *New Africa* (London), May 1983.

44. Theo Malan, "Regional Economic Cooperation in Southern Africa," *African Insight* 13 (1983), 48.

45. W.B. Holtes, "The Future of Trade between the Republic of South Africa and Black Africa," *ISSUP Strategic Review* (August 1983), 3.

46. Data supplied by the South African Foreign Trade Organisation.

47. Ibid.

48. Malan, "Regional," 78.

49. Trade creation is regarded as a benefit of customs unions. If industries in partner countries are not competitive, there is trade diversion (a high-cost supplier from within the customs union supplants a low-cost source outside), and this is a cost. Nevertheless, for long-term, intra-union trade the industries of partner countries should have the potential to become complementary. Since SADCC is not a customs union, trade would be facilitated by the existence of complementary industries (as explained in the previous paragraph).

50. *Sunday Tribune,* 3 October and 17 October 1982. More recently, the two countries concluded discussions on a trade agreement, and the clothing industry apparently was an important issue. See *Botswana Daily News,* 30 April 1984.

51. Ibid., 24 January 1982, and *Daily News* (Durban), 8 January 1982.

52. Hill, "Regional," 222.

53. See *African Business,* January 1983.

54. *Africa Report,* May–June 1983.

55. *The Herald,* 13 September 1983.

56. Kingdom of Lesotho, *Third Five-year Development Plan 1980/1981–1984/85,* 83.

57. Nsekela, *Africa,* 197.

58. C.W. Stahl and W.R. Bohning, "Reducing Dependence on Migration in Southern Africa" in W.R. Bohning (ed.), *Black Migration to South Africa* (Geneva, 1981), 158.

59. Gavin G. Maasdorp, "Reassessing Economic Ties in Southern Africa," *Optima,* 30 (1981), 125. A common market involves the free movement of factors of production among member countries.

60. Nsekela, *Africa,* 198.

61. Ibid., 199.

62. Ibid., 205. See also *African Business* (October 1982), for a recent assessment of unemployment problems in southern Africa.

63. Usually referred to as SATS. This is incorrect: This acronym is in long-standing use by a mutual fund, and the South African Transport Services is obliged to use "SAT."

64. A study by Earl L. McFarland, quoted in Arne Tostensen, *Dependence and Collective Self-reliance in Southern Africa* (Uppsala, 1982), 29.

65. Power failures on the ESCOM grid therefore affect these countries; e.g., in November 1983 a massive power failure hit large parts of South Africa as well as Botswana, Lesotho, and Mozambique. *Natal Mercury* (Durban), 26 November 1983.

66. Ibid., 28 March 1983.

67. Calculated from official statistical bulletins in these countries.

68. Following Tostensen, *Dependence,* 16–20.

69. Anglin, "SADCC," 29–31.

70. *African Business* (August and September 1982).

71. Agence France Press, 3 February 1984.

72. Leys and Tostensen, "Regional," 68.

73. Peter Vale, "Hawks, Doves and Regional Strategy," *The Star* (Johannesburg), 3 September 1982. In retrospect, however, the differences may not have been so clear-cut; there may well have been (and probably still are) shades of cross-cutting opinion with differences regarding emphasis and timing.

74. J.G.H. Loubser, "Transport Co-operation in Southern Africa," *ISSUP Strategic Review* (Pretoria), (November 1982); *Sunday Tribune,* 10 October 1982.

75. "Extract, concerning the loan of locomotives to Zimbabwe, from a Statement in Parliament by the South African Minister of Transport Affairs, the Hon. H. Schoeman, on 22 September 1981," *Southern Africa Record* (25–26 December 1981), 18–20. In January 1983, Pretoria also insisted that fuel talks be held at government level with Zimbabwe after the destruction of storage tanks in Beira. *Daily News,* 7 January 1983.

76. See *The Economist* (16 July 1983), 15, 23.

77. G.M.E. Leistner, "Regional Cooperation as a Cornerstone of South African External Policy," *Africa Insight 13* (1983), 4.

78. A good account of the MNR is contained in André Thomashausen, "The National Resistance of Mozambique," *Africa Insight 13* (1983), 125–129.

79. Deon Geldenhuys, "The Destabilisation Controversy: An Analysis of a High-Risk Foreign Policy Option for South Africa," *South African Journal of Political Science IX* (December 1982), 220. See also Rotberg, "Introduction," above, 8–9.

80. Geldenhuys, "Analysis," 20–21.

81. Douglas G. Anglin, "The Frontline States and the Future of Southern Africa," Paper presented at a conference on "The Indian Ocean: Perspectives on a Strategic Arena," Dalhousie University (1982), 32.

82. See *Southern Africa Record 35* (1984), for full records of the text. It is interesting to note that the Accord contains what Deon Geldenhuys had referred to as the "rules of the game" that Pretoria was trying to establish. These are: (1) disallowing insurgents the use of one's territory as a base for attacking one's neighbor; (2) ceasing material support for rebel or liberation movements; and (3) continuing normal economic ties despite political differences. See his "South Africa's Regional Policy," Paper presented at Golden Jubilee Conference of the South African Institute of Race Relations (1984), 33.

83. Reproduced in the *Botswana Daily News* 2 May 1984.

84. *Daily News,* 30 April 1984. President Kaunda, in an interview with *Leadership SA 3* (1984), 17, had expressed his willingness to host such a meeting.

85. *Swazi Observer,* 7 May 1984.

86. *Times of Swaziland,* 14 May 1984. See also *South African Digest,* 6 April 1984.

87. *Sunday Tribune,* 13 May 1984.

88. *Botswana Daily News,* 14 May 1984.

89. *Sunday Times* (Johannesburg), 15 April 1984.

90. *Natal Mercury,* 25 April 1984.

91. See ibid., 26 February 1984; *Financial Mail* (Johannesburg), 16 March 1984.

92. *Natal Mercury,* 25 April 1984.

93. *Financial Mail,* 16 March 1984.

94. See article by Arthur Hammond-Tooke, *Sunday Times,* 18 March 1984.

95. *Africa Economic Digest,* 4 February 1983.

96. Ibid., 10 February 1984.

97. *Africa Now,* March 1983. One of these alleged contradictions is that among the major donors are those Western countries most strongly tied to South Africa and with most interest in maintaining a strong South African economy. Western support for SADCC has been interpreted as "an alibi to cover up their relationship with South Africa . . . it is tempting for donor countries to regard support for southern Africa as an alternative to stiffer action against South Africa, i.e., the imposition of effective sanctions" (Leys and Tostensen, "Regional," 69).

98. Ibid.

99. See, for example, the issues of 11 February 1984, 76, and 24 March 1984, 13.

100. *Times of Swaziland,* 21 October 1983.

101. Ibid., 23 September 1982.

102. *Angola Information Bulletin,* 25 July 1983; *Africa Now,* September 1983.

103. Agence France Press, 27 October 1983, quoting the vice-president of Tanzania speaking at a conference of SADCC trade and industry ministers.

104. *Daily News,* 12 April 1984.

105. *Africa Research Bulletin,* 15 October–14 November 1983.

7

Namibia: The Regional Stalemate

Robert I. Rotberg

I n the mid-1980s Namibia still remained a part of South Africa. That it had not been launched toward independence testified as much to the complexity of the Namibian problem as it did to the growth in South African power and the failure of constructive engagement as an effective instrument of change. Namibia had become strategically central to the future of the southern African region; thus a solution to the Namibian issue depended more and more on a resolution of regional questions, and on South Africa's ultimate place in the region.

The carrots of constructive engagement had provided little definitive leverage on Namibia by late 1984 precisely because U.S. policy had been focused on the narrow goal itself rather than on that same goal as an integral part of a comprehensive, regional objective. Clarity on the two key issues—South Africa's own future and its role as a regional power— had been subordinated to the achievement of tactical, if worthy, advances. Furthermore, an altered context of global as well as regional realities had given constructive engagement less salience and South Africa relatively more power compared to other local and international participants. In 1985 progress toward an internationally negotiated transformation of Namibia, from a lapsed mandatory territory into a new, universally recognized nation, appeared just as difficult as it had throughout the early 1980s.

Namibia, a land twice the size of California, is seven-eighths desert and semidesert, with only its northern hinterland receiving crop-sustaining regular refreshments of rain. Nearly two-thirds of all Namibians, especially the dominant Ovambo and their Kavango and Caprivi neighbors, live in this northern sphere, traditionally growing sorghum, pulses, and—recently—maize amid the palm trees south of the Kunene and Kavango rivers. The Ovambo number about 600,000, the Kavango 100,000 and the Caprivi 40,000. In the arid west are 11,000 Kaokovelders. Many Ovambo have become labor migrants, working either in the territory's mines, in its few cities and towns, or on farms owned by others.

Central Namibia contains both Windhoek, the capital and the only main city (pop. 120,000); a number of small towns; and—on the Atlantic coast—both Swakopmund, a Hanseatic, German-appearing and sounding touristic center and, nearby, the South African enclave of Walvis Bay, Namibia's only real port. This central belt of the country is the home of about 83,000 Damara and 76,000 Herero, as well as 40,000 Coloureds (recent emigrants from South Africa) and nearly all of Namibia's 70,000 whites (10,000 English-speakers, 25,000 German-speakers, with the remainder using Afrikaans as a mother tongue). Of the whites, only 4,000 farm. Most are employed in the civil service or by the South African–run railways, airways, and other state bodies. About 9,000 Tswana and 35,000 San (Bushmen) live in the eastern sections of this central region.

Southern Namibia—from Rehoboth to the Orange River border with South Africa—is a dry grazing area inhabited by 45,000 brown-skinned Nama (nineteenth-century conquerors from South Africa), 25,000 similarly brown-skinned Baster farmers who live in and around Rehoboth (the Basters also came from South Africa), and a few thousand whites.

In the far south, at the mouth of the Orange River, Namibia mines gem diamonds. Taxes on these exports of the Consolidated Diamond Mines, a wholly owned subsidiary of the De Beers Ltd. cartel of South Africa, in 1984 contributed about 20 percent of the tax revenue of Namibia (an annual total of about R1 billion). Although diamonds may in the future play a somewhat less crucial role than they now do in the country's economy, it is hard to conceive of a modern Namibia that in this century does not live largely on their glittering proceeds.[1]

There is coal, too, in Namibia's south; but it is not of high enough quality to be exploitable in today's market. Instead, second to diamonds, is the 5,000 tons or so of yellowcake—uranium oxide—which is dug each year out of a mountain east of Swakopmund by a company controlled by Rio Tinto Zinc of Britain. (There are Canadian, French, and South African partners.) Although the world spot price of yellowcake was at mid-decade too low to justify new mining of uranium in Namibia, the present operation had long-term contracts sufficient to make uranium a key contributor to Namibia's state revenues (about 10 percent) and to its GNP throughout the remainder of the 1980s.

Copper, cadmium, lead, zinc, and arsenic—mined at Tsumeb and elsewhere in the country's central region—commanded such low world prices in the first half of the 1980s that as national revenue producers or profit-making enterprises they had become unimportant. There are small tin mines, too. Only Tsumeb is a sizable enterprise, but it has returned little to its U.S. owners (primarily Newmont Mining), or to its South African partners, since the middle 1970s.

Namibia once caught and canned fish, but the large schools of sardines and pilchards that earlier came to Walvis Bay were overfished and may not reappear in this century. The market, largely West German, for the skins of karakul sheep, also receded as a result of recession and changes in fashion. Namibia has never slaughtered much of its cattle, and its abbatoirs are small. Nor has there been much internal production of food staples for interregional sale.

As an economic entity, Namibia is highly geared, with an outstanding infrastructure and a first-rate service system for a country of small population and limited potential. The South African connection has clearly contributed to this modernity, giving Windhoek and the other towns a striking aspect in the midst of an arid and semiarid grazing zone. But Namibia imports 70 percent of its food (predominantly from South Africa) and virtually all its consumer durables. It adds little value to its major raw-material exports, all of which are ultimately sold in the Northern Hemisphere.

If world markets for base metals improve dramatically over the next two decades, Namibian resources could be exploited more than at present. But the costs of proving new deposits under 50 meters of Kalahari sand are high. Likewise, known hills of uranium could be exported if world prices doubled. Failing these improbabilities, and absent the return of sardines and pilchards, Namibia will remain no unusually rich prize. Nor will it prosper except through the continued production and export of diamonds and uranium (the two largest employers of local labor), an attempt to raise and slaughter more beef and sheep, and—if the terms of rural trade can be arranged satisfactorily—major new attention being devoted to the production of maize and rice for local consumption.

In addition to these several factors, which limit Namibia's future growth, the country's most grievous impediment is its shortage of trained indigenous manpower. Because of German (to 1915) and South African failures to provide educational opportunities for the peoples of the territory, there were at mid-decade no more than 350 black Namibians who had graduated from a recognized university. There was one black lawyer and five black physicians, and a sprinkling of other trained professionals or technically qualified indigenous individuals. Indeed, in recent years, fewer than 100 indigenous Namibians have matriculated (graduated) annually from secondary school.

Politically, there are two Namibias. Since the mid-1960s, the South West African People's Organization (SWAPO) has been the only indigenous party of national and international salience. Founded as an Ovambo group in the late 1950s and as SWAPO in 1960, it was anti–South African and Western-backed until about 1971, when it turned for funds and arms to the Soviet Union. Since then, and especially in the late 1970s,

SWAPO has attempted to oust South Africa from Namibia by force, raiding first across the Zambezi River into the Caprivi region of Namibia from Zambia, and then—after South Africa attacked Zambia and Angola became independent—from bases in Angola between the upper reaches of the Kunene and Kavango Rivers. These guerrilla attacks have successfully disturbed northern Namibia as far south as Grootfontein and Tsumeb. Since the mid-1970s, South Africa has used 25,000 or more troops to defend its presence in Namibia and, in recent years, to push SWAPO well back into Angola as well.

In terms of battlefield strength, SWAPO probably can count about 3,000–5,000 trained guerrillas, down from 12,000 a year or two ago, and logistical support from the Angolan army, Cuban troops in Angola, and Soviet and East German advisers.[2] Its arms have been no match for those of South Africa, nor can it interfere more than sporadically with South African control of the skies of southern Angola and northern Namibia. Yet as pronounced as is South African military might in the area, SWAPO is a guerrilla movement and continues to infiltrate small groups into Namibia. There they mine roads, bomb administrative buildings, and assassinate collaborators. Weakened SWAPO certainly was as an insurgent force in 1983 and 1984; defeated it was not, and probably can never be. Nor—given conditions like those of today—can it ever bleed Namibia as thoroughly as the Patriotic Front did so dramatically in Rhodesia. SWAPO is unlikely to win the independence of Namibia by warfare.

Yet as weak as SWAPO has become militarily, it remains the only Namibian political entity with unchallengable legitimacy. Inside Namibia its organization is admittedly much more flaccid than it once was; some of its leaders are discredited, others have been detained or have fled. Yet just as the African National Congress is still regarded by black South Africans as the only credible liberation movement in South Africa, so the standing of SWAPO has no equal inside Namibia. Bolstered by South Africa's vigorous opposition on the battlefield and by the number of times that South Africa's white leadership has called it the enemy, SWAPO has reserves of political strength among potential Ovambo, Kavango, Damara, and Nama voters. Even Herero, who traditionally have been anti-Ovambo, are well represented among the upper ranks of the SWAPO official hierarchy.

SWAPO's legitimacy was strengthened considerably in mid-1984, when South Africa finally released Andimba Toivo ja Toivo, SWAPO's founder, from prison after sixteen years. Although South Africa may have expected Toivo to assist its own attempts to obtain an internal solution to the Namibian problem, Toivo was soon elected secretary-general of SWAPO. He has since played a loyal second to Sam Nujoma,

SWAPO's fiery president, at negotiating sessions with South Africa in Zambia and Cape Verde, and in New York and London, and took an uncompromising position in opposition to the policies and pretensions of South Africa in Namibia. During the course of an interview, he blamed the Reagan administration for consistently hampering progress toward Namibian independence: "The so-called constructive engagement policy has served to camouflage Washington's open embrace of the oppressive apartheid regime. Washington's preoccupation is to keep southern Africa safe for continued plunder of natural resources, and unmitigated exploitation of labour. This selfish interest has led the Reagan Administration actively to support Pretoria in continuing its illegal and brutal occupation of Namibia."[3]

Serious political alternatives to SWAPO are not now apparent. Although the once significant Democratic Turnhalle Alliance (DTA) remains in existence, its support among potential black voters is as weak as its appeal everywhere continues questionable. As an amalgam of black and brown local groups led by an Afrikaner and supported from its inception in 1977 by South Africa, the DTA always had a problem countering SWAPO's inherent and historic appeal. This became more and more apparent, especially to South Africa, leading early in 1983 to a final public rupture between South Africa and the DTA. Namibians and South Africa no longer regard the DTA as a prime vehicle for countering SWAPO in elections.

South Africa can now admit that no political grouping to which it gives birth and which it backs morally and financially will prove viable in Namibia in this decade. Theoretically, South Africa thus ought to declare that a new political era has commenced, and should begin readying the territory for its eventual emergence as a black, doubtless SWAPO-ruled, state. Making such a transition meaningful would increase the likelihood that Namibia and South Africa could develop a mutually agreeable relationship as weak and strong neighboring nations after independence. As a result of domestic South African white political considerations, however, South African military successes, the diminished costs of a failure to please the West, and the political disarray within Namibia (and the lack of any viable indigenous alternative to SWAPO), South Africa cannot yet contemplate or accept the utility of such an alternative.

Instead, from 1983 South Africa has tried without success to fashion a new internal political formula that could provide an alternative to the process of change prescribed by Security Council Resolution 435. It tried to collect representatives of the major political groups within the territory into a national council that would make recommendations about the future constitutional development of the territory, the result constituting an "authentic" Namibian voice. However, few of the local political parties, particularly the black-led ones, were prepared to accept nomination to such a council.[4]

A plethora of other non-SWAPO Namibian political parties still exist, most of which are and have been opposed to South African control of Namibia. They each disapproved of the DTA and cooperated as little as possible with South Africa. Nearly all have come to accept the salience of SWAPO while eschewing the use of violence as a means to the mutually desired end of independence. Few any more reckon that alone or in combination they would emerge from a national election with a decisive bloc of votes.

From a historic point of view, the most important of these intermediate organizations is the South West African National Union (SWANU), which had Chinese and radical chic support throughout the 1960s. Now, however, it is a local organization with a predominantly Herero membership. Led first by Moses Katjiuongua and then by Nora Chase, in 1984 the Chase segment became realistic in its public view of SWAPO. Ottilie Abrahams, Chase's sister, and Dr. Kenneth Abrahams, her husband, run the very small Namibian Independence party. SWAPO-Democrats (SWAPO-D), an equally tiny unit, is led by Andreas Shipanga, an Ovambo who rose to very high rank in SWAPO before breaking with the SWAPO hierarchy in 1976.[5] John Kirkpatrick and Brian O'Linn led the tiny white Federal party. Together, most of these groups, along with the Damara Council, once were linked loosely as the Namibian National Front (NNF). But the council now runs the second-tier (regional) Damara government and has retreated from the national scene; and the NNF is moribund. Additionally, each ethnic group or locality in Namibia is represented by one or more political vehicles of personal or group expression, but none is of national significance.

During 1983 and 1984 several of these organizations formed the Multi-Party Conference (MPC) and attempted to become a successful broker between South Africa and SWAPO. Despite dissent within SWANU, Katjiuongua's part of SWANU tried with little success to forge an alliance of internal parties which could accelerate the implementation of Resolution 435. The MPC took part in the Lusaka conference of 1984, which brought SWAPO, the Namibian administration, and the MPC together for the first time; but no agreement could be achieved.

Internally, Namibia in 1985 constituted a political vacuum. SWAPO had revitalized its presence inside the territory by selecting Pastor Hendrik Witbooi, a distinguished Nama leader, as its organizational vice-president and titular chief. Otherwise, and despite a flurry of maneuvering connected with the attempt to appoint an interim government, such initiative as remained largely rested with South Africa's administrator-general. In accord with South African policy, he was continuing to avoid the political modernization of Namibia. He had refrained from altering the existing governmental direction of the territory and thus from weakening the power of the right-wing white parties. Instead of opting to prepare Namibia for independnece in an expeditious manner by abolishing the framework of regional government that had strengthened ethnic identities and, particularly, given local whites control over educational, medical, and other services that would otherwise have been subject to multiracial influence, the administrator-general supported the status quo. By 1985 he had taken no steps to extend the scope and hasten the pace of desegregation. He had also initiated no bold moves to accelerate the education and training of Africans or to promote economic development, especially in northern Namibia.

As an agent of South Africa, the administrator-general's innovations in the early 1980s were tactical, not strategic. His mandate did not visibly include the readying of Namibia for a U.N.-sponsored form of independence. In that sense, and absent any major new policy departures from South Africa, the fate of Namibia will continue to be decided upon elsewhere—primarily in Pretoria and Luanda, and at a succession of international negotiating tables.

Despite much *sturm und drang,* the negotiations themselves were stalled throughout 1981–1984. Yet in terms of the modalities of an overall settlement, or even the details of each modality, little separated South Africa from SWAPO and the Western Contact Group (the U.S., Britain, France, West Germany, and Canada). Agreement on many items had been reached before the Carter administration left office. Its successor, ultimately hewing to the guidelines of Security Council Resolution 435, worked out a compromise over constitutional principles and the form of an eventual "free and fair," internationally validated, national election for a Namibian constituent assembly. The deployment, the numbers, and the approximate composition of the putative United Nations truce administering force was known. So were the numbers and dispositions of the South African troops who would remain during a transition period. The time periods between agreement and the stages of implementation were fixed. True, fine points still needed to be discussed, questions about the command and control of U.N. and South African forces required answers, the logistics of the exercise—never easy across such remote distances—needed to be planned, and the required funds were still to be found.

But as close as the several sides may have been over these and other issues, the negotiations in a real sense remained in a phase of permanent pause—as they had often been—because South Africa was in no hurry to settle and, indeed, could not afford to agree to any simple conclusion to the Namibian question. To this long-term obstacle was added a further impediment: the presence of Cuban troops in nearby Angola.

Cuban troops came to Angola in 1975 to assist the Soviet-backed Movement for the Popular Liberation of Angola (MPLA) in its struggle for victory in Angola against two Western-supported armies: the Front for the National Liberation of Angola and the Union for the Total Independence of Angola (UNITA). The Cubans helped the MPLA counter a short-lived South African invasion of Angola, also in 1975. At mid-decade, 30,600 Cuban soldiers still defend the MPLA government against UNITA (which has a secure base in southeastern Angola and is supplied and assisted by South Africa) and provide some logistical backing for SWAPO. They do little to help defend southern Angola from South African preemptive attacks; but their presence, together with that of the Angolan army, deters South African raids on central and northern Angola.

From 1982 the United States and South Africa linked the exodus of Cuban troops from Angola to decisive progress on a settlement of the Namibian problem. The removal of the Cubans would be seen to increase South Africa's sense of security in the southern African region. At least, that is an assertion that can be argued plausibly, objective appraisals of known strategic balances to the contrary. The Cuban removal would also weaken the MPLA and would therefore strengthen UNITA. An ideal arrangement, from the South African perspective, would be a takeover of the Angolan government by UNITA. Short of that transformation, the South Africans expect, once the Cuban shield is removed, that a place will be found in the Angolan government for UNITA. They also assume, which perhaps they should not, that UNITA will remain pro–South African and antagonistic to the ideological goals toward which most African states incline. In terms of Namibia, a diminution of the Cuban presence would permit South Africa to regard any electoral victory of SWAPO with greater equanimity. If SWAPO won and the Cubans were still in Angola, the argument goes, the red flag would fly dangerously over Windhoek, and Cubans in Namibia would pose an immediate threat to the security of South Africa itself.

The advantages that, it is claimed, would derive from a Cuban withdrawal are strategic. The major advantage for the South Africans, however, would be psychological. A Cuban exodus would support the government of South Africa's image as a negotiator obdurate enough to preserve white South Africa against external danger. Once the Cubans went, President Pieter W. Botha's South African government could end its control of Namibia without worrying too much about adverse domestic political fallout, or about accusations that it had handed the territory, and the whites there, over to Marxism. Its inability to devise an effective internal political counterweight to SWAPO would be seen to be less fatal.

Another view suggests that these various pleadings are more or less irrelevant. A Cuban withdrawal is linked, by South Africa anyway, to the effective settlement of the Namibian question largely because the likelihood of such an outcome is remote. Although the Angolans have time and again said that they want the Cubans to go—and although there are good economic and political reasons that their government should, in fact, want the Cubans to leave—without a satisfactory prior elimination of, or accommodation to, the threat from UNITA, the present government of Angola would risk its very existence if the Cubans departed.

Bilateral direct talks between Angola and South Africa, which have been held intermittently since late 1982, need not be seen in the context of a settlement. Construed as a separate initiative, leading to a possible cease-fire, the talks in 1984 produced benefits for both South Africa and Angola, isolated SWAPO, strengthened UNITA, and may have led away from—not toward—a resolution of the larger struggle for Namibia. Given the extent to which South Africa gained mastery in 1982–1983 over southern Angola and has so thoroughly hamstrung the attacking ability of SWAPO, it was in Angola's interest to end hostilities. Otherwise, Angola can exercise little effective hegemony over its southern reaches. With an end to the war, South African raids will presumably halt, and Angola can gradually assert itself to the farthest points of its own domain. Likewise, with SWAPO leashed, South Africa can pull back to the Namibian border and compel Angola to undertake the policing of SWAPO.

The cease-fire of 1984 thus acknowledged South Africa's current position of strategic superiority, diminished the stature of the Cubans, gave the image of the South African government a psychological boost, and deflected attention from the main settlement negotiations themselves. Moreover, behind the cessation of hostilities and the virtual end of guerrilla threat to Namibia, South Africa became ideally placed to pursue the possibility of some kind of internal settlement. Whether or not those are South Africa's intentions, it should be clear that the cease-fire runs along the second of the two tracks that have long been followed by South Africa's negotiators. Furthermore, the cease-fire profoundly strengthened South Africa's international bargaining position.

South Africa, as a presumed rational actor in a rational world, should want to bring the long-running Namibian soap opera to an end. Large sums of expenditure could be foregone; the war on the border is estimated to cost at least $2 billion a year. Additional opportunity costs lost include the time underutilized by conscripts whose efforts could more productively be employed at home; industrial capacity diverted to armaments and other supplies of war; and the diversion of logistical resources away from the civilian economy of the Republic and the region. The large budgeted sums saved could be devoted to underfinanced national needs, such as the expansion of black educational and training facilities; the raising of salaries in the black educational sector; and, say, the development of the impoverished rural homelands.

Although South African losses in the war have been few, eliminating the likelihood of casualties would still have widespread appeal in the white community of the Republic. The border conflict cannot yet be considered unpopular, but only in a few quarters is it regarded as a fully just war. From admittedly impressionistic evidence, it appears that white South Africans—the current electorate—are less worried about the potential dangers of a black-run Namibia than are their political leaders. Already the impact of an independent black Namibia has been discounted. Namibia is still remote, across a vast, largely uninhabited desert from the main South African population centers in the Transvaal, and north a long way across equally harsh terrain from Cape Town.

The West wants a Namibian settlement. Agreeing to it would, it has long been assumed, embellish South Africa's image in Western eyes and result in tangible as well as psychological benefits for South Africa. But South Africa blocks such progress. There would also be domestic political advantages to be gained by removing Namibia from the list of international disputes. The proposition is also advanced that South Africa can cut its best deal—indeed, its only favorable deal—over Namibia only so long as the Reagan administration is in office. A less constructively engaged U.S. adversary would give South Africa poorer terms when and if South Africa decides or is compelled to loosen its hold on Namibia. Within the Republic, too, politicians note that settling the Namibian issue becomes more and more controversial the nearer in time it is to a South African election.

These are reasonable arguments that should help concentrate South Africa's official mind on a devolution of power in Namibia. However, there are countervailing axioms; they seem to have held South Africa to its negative course despite the many explicit and the many more implicit carrots of constructive engagement. Anxiety in the National party about potential domestic political disgruntlement if Namibia becomes or seems to be becoming a SWAPO-dominated state is a factor. The widespread acknowledgment that SWAPO today has a likely marked electoral edge only accentuates that anxiety. No reassurances by Western observers about SWAPO's actual Marxist commitment and no intelligence estimates of the extent to which a SWAPO government would work effectively with South Africa in the postindependence era have dampened the official enthusiasm to categorize SWAPO as pernicious, its leaders as the devils incarnate, and so on.

At least one influential group of South African decision makers is determined to permit an internationally validated election in Namibia only when a surrogate political party has somehow developed sufficient popular appeal to counter the undeniable attraction of SWAPO. Despite the demise of the DTA and the weakness of the MPC alternative, the military and some of the politicians concerned with Namibia still wish to create such a client, even if to do so from scratch will obviously take several years.

There is less sentiment at mid-decade than before to move South African battle lines south from the Angolan border to South Africa's frontier along the Orange River with Namibia. The military has demonstrated its ability to pursue an Israeli-style strategy of retaliation and preemption; politicians are comfortable for the most part with its unexpected success. For at least a year or two they foresee few hindrances to the pursuit of such a policy; the West has complained only mildly, the Soviets and Soviet proxies are not spoiling for a fight, and the Angolans (as well as SWAPO) have been sufficiently weakened to embolden the most ambitious of the architects of South Africa's forward policy. South Africa has even achieved a separate peace which has deescalated hostilities, saved costs, given South Africa enormous psychological advantages, and provided a wall of time behind which to pursue the surrogate option.

Most of all, South Africa has several serious incentives for deferring a settlement as long as possible. The Reagan administration's tactics have given South Africa more freedom to pursue a policy of tactical realignment at home and destabilization abroad than was possible in the Carter years. By this logic, agreeing to a conclusion of the Namibian imbroglio makes no sense; immediately Namibia ceases to be an issue of international concern, the West will—a fortiori—focus its attention on South Africa itself. This turn South Africa wants to avoid as long as possible. The argument that a subsequent U.S. administration, or even this one, annoyed, will deal differently with South Africa is a risk that—given the success of South Africa's bargaining tactics since 1977—is thought to be worth running. The costs of doing nothing while sheltering behind the bogey of a Cuban presence in Angola are perceived to be less, probably far less, than the risks of giving up an advantage without clear gain. The fruits of Western gratitude cannot be sweet enough, for only the kinds of guarantees that no Western government could give to white South Africa would substitute for the broad power that South Africa continues to derive from its control of Namibia.

White-ruled South Africa wants to ensure its short- and long-term security. Western pressure for change internally, when combined with urban unrest and/or an escalating equilibrium of violence, poses the major threat to the perpetuation of white hegemony. (The Soviet threat is largely derivative, a function of the maintenance of apartheid and the failure to find viable channels for black political participation.) This being so, it is profoundly in South Africa's white self-interest to focus the attention of the West on Namibia. In this light, Namibia's main value to South Africa is as a psychological buffer—an object of bargaining contention. South Africa therefore gives up the position of bargainer in the great game of Namibia only at its own peril, or only when Namibia has outlived its usefulness to South Africa as a high-card flush.[6] When Rhodesia was still an issue internationally, the question of Namibia seemed easier to resolve—and it was, because the West needed South Africa's help in that arena. Today, only the existence of the Namibian problem keeps the West from South Africa's door. What, then, is the overriding South African incentive to settle?

Constructive engagement has reinforced South Africa's appreciation of its bargaining advantages. Instead of incentives, linking the Cubans to the process and withholding dramatic démarches about destabilization has given South Africa every reason to strengthen its borders and to negotiate a separate peace with Angola rather than the comprehensive settlement the West wants.

South Africa and the United States have interests in Namibia that diverge fundamentally. The West wants to eliminate a potential source of East-West conflict by taking Namibia to independence. It also wants to strengthen ties to the nations of black Africa by fostering Namibia's transformation. Overall, it sees the achievement of Namibia's independence as the primary means of bringing stability to an otherwise volatile region. Stability is essential for economic development and political progress. Its spread also deprives the Soviet Union of new opportunities to fish in the turbulent waters of discontent, and could also make the Cuban contribution less conclusive. The South Africans, however—erroneously from the U.S. view, but nevertheless vitally—regard stability as inimical to their own existence as a white-ruled country. Black peace and prosperity on the South African periphery is seen to weaken the case for continued white tutelage within South Africa itself. There is an unsubstantiated notion that successes in the neighboring states will encourage South Africa's own black population. Emulation, backed by the West, could be dangerous for the survival of white South Africa.

The West wants to close the Namibian case. Constructive engagers have said that South Africa needs the United States and therefore must, especially during this administration, produce results. The South Africans, however, no longer fear a U.S. retreat from the bargaining table.

Too much is at stake for the State Department; too much has been invested. And South Africa never says no. It simply buries its reluctance behind the Cubans as it once cried U.N. impartiality. Moreover, since it is at least arguable that South Africa's fundamental interest is never to settle and incessantly to bargain—always to be wanted and never to concede—a process characterized by constant wooing can succeed only if there are major shifts in South Africa's assessment of its available options.

How to effect that reassessment, a Cuban exit or no, is the foreign-policy dilemma of the later 1980s. Arguably, constructive engagement might still succeed if it is fine-tuned, if the carrots are withdrawn and a few sticks are brandished. But constructive engagement was by 1985 a posture composed of a series of omissions and commissions. Altering the overall approach could well depend upon a basic reevaluation of the importance of the Cape sea route, of the minerals of South Africa, of South Africa's value to the Free World—indeed, of the whole notion of South Africa's strategic significance to the West. If those issues were placed in a fresh perspective, which has not been the hallmark of the Reagan administration, and if South Africa's own true self-perception of its own self-interest became fully appreciated, then and only then could the impress of U.S. needs be brought productively to bear on South Africa, and therefore on the question of Namibia. Implicit in this for-mulation is the setting of U.S. goals in a regional, even African, context. What is good for the United States, and what assists our global goals, is not a cozy relationship with South Africa. It is also arguable that such a cozy relationship retards South Africa's pursuit of those very goals of substantial reform that are at last seen to be in its own overriding self-interest.

Notes

1. For details on the economy and political economy of modern Namibia, see Wolfgang Thomas, "The Economy in Transition to Independence," in Rob-ert I. Rotberg (ed.), *Namibia: Political and Economic Prospects* (Lexington, 1983), 41–91.

2. *The Star Weekly*, 8 January 1983.

3. Quoted in Victoria Brittain, "A Hundred Years of Struggle," *The Guardian*, 14 September 1984.

4. Rotberg, "Stalemate in Namibian Soap Opera," *Southern Africa Report*, I (1983), 1–2.

5. For details, see Rotberg, *Suffer the Future: Policy Choices in Southern Africa* (Cambridge, Mass., 1980), 210–211.

6. Rotberg, "Political and Economic Realities in a Time of Settlement," in idem (ed.), *Namibia*, 38–40.

8
The Dynamics of Southern Africa and U.S. Policy

Robert I. Rotberg

Of all the obvious violent conflicts of contemporary Africa—the struggle for Chad, the battle for the soul of Ethiopia and its hinterland, the civil war in Uganda, the civil war in the Sudan, and the long-running competition in the Western Sahara—none is more consuming and more in desperate need of a new United States policy than the enormously bitter, globalized, and reputedly cataclysmic conflict between white supremacy and majority black aspirations in southern Africa.

Included within the parameters of this confrontation are the struggles for primacy in Angola and Mozambique, the contentious but less encompassing battles in Lesotho and Swaziland, the much more muted but still dangerous affray in Zimbabwe, the war for Namibia, and the central conflict in South Africa. It is this last antagonism around which the others revolve, and to which they all—and much else in the southern half of Africa—relate. Each has been fueled by the heat of the core conflict; each continues to attract the attention of the United States (as well as that of the Soviet Union) and the West as potential sources of global rivalry as well as regional instability. Overriding each situation, and at the very nucleus of the South African dilemma itself, is the perpetuation of the fundamental inequality—and the consequent tensions—that stem from apartheid and the maldistribution of power.

The conflict in South and southern Africa is different in character than those elsewhere in Africa. Elsewhere, black elites, sometimes supported by external forces, vie for power, access to power, and autonomy (escape from power). But the South African struggle, and thus the surrounding and related battles, is for respect, dignity, participation, privilege, human rights, and civil liberty, as well as access to and the wielding of power in its rawest form.

The making of U.S. policy respecting a struggle that has close analogies to our own ought to prove easy. But it has instead been enormously difficult; for South Africa, albeit white-ruled and afflicted with the cancer of apartheid, is a strong nation, rich in resources, locally dominant, Western in character and alignment, and historically an associate of the West. Moreover, the United States has long traded with and invested in South Africa. Despite the obvious injustice of apartheid, the United States has been both reluctant and unable to abandon ties and influence or to attack blindly without knowing what would follow. The United States wonders whether or not moral repugnance offers a solid and sustainable basis for the development of workable U.S. policies. Furthermore, the precise location of U.S. self-interest has always been in question. So has efficacy: If the test of self-interest could be met, would the policy succeed in changing South Africa for the better—presumably making it more humane and just, and providing for the fuller participation in power of the majority?

The nature of the conflict in South Africa is well known and is little changed in essentials. South Africa is permanently at war. Its 22 million Africans are subordinated politically, economically, socially, educationally, medically, and in every other conceivable way to the 4.7 million whites who rule South Africa as they have ruled it since the seventeenth century. In addition, the whites control the destinies of 2.6 million Coloureds (persons of mixed white and black descent) and 800,000 Asians, who are regarded by the South African government as nonwhite and who fill out the demographic profile of the troubled country.

The war for South Africa has several aspects. Whites, recognizing the enormous disparity between their own and African numbers, fear the kind of shifts in power in their country that would diminish their own preeminence and/or transfer even a scintilla of prerogative to Africans. Thus whites, who have always controlled the governments of South Africa, refuse to give Africans a vote in the national political arena; limit African freedom of movement from the countryside to the town or among towns; make them carry and produce identity documents or passes; closely regulate where they can live, be educated, worship, how they can travel, and with whom they may cohabit. For the same reason the white government denies Africans citizenship in South Africa, and has created ten homelands where Africans supposedly may enjoy political and other privileges. The combination of laws that subject Africans to white-determined rules is collectively called *apartheid*, or separation. Other nations oppress their own people, and discriminate against them in one or more ways, but South Africa is the only one that does so exclusively on the basis of color.

Coloureds and Asians are also subject to nearly all of the exactions of apartheid, with an important qualified exception. In 1984 the white government changed its form from one with a Westminster parliament and a ceremonial president to one headed by an executive president and a legislature consisting of a tricameral parliament with one dominant house for whites and weaker houses for Coloureds and Asians. Coloureds and Asians now vote, but only for representatives to their own racial chambers. Africans still are denied the vote, except for local officials in the homelands and in some color-restricted cities.

The other side of the war is black resistance to white domination and subjection. There is sullen, passive rejection of whites, which occurs every day. There is public criticism of the government by a number of harassed but functional political groups like the United Democratic Front, the Azanian People's Organization (AZAPO), the Soweto Civic Association, the Forum, and so on. Within the white parliament, too, the Progressive Federal party attacks the apartheid policies of the ruling National party. But the major indigenous opponent of white rule is the long-banned African National Congress (ANC), a Soviet-backed guerrilla movement that infiltrates South Africa from outside and periodically sabotages government-owned or government-related installations. Since 1977 the number of incidents has multiplied two-hundred-fold, many insurgents have been captured and tried, and South Africa has increased its antiguerrilla patrols; but the spate of attacks on property, and occasionally on individuals, continues largely unabated.

The clash between white and black is for South Africa, but it is not yet a clash of culture (since both sides are Western), of religion (both are more or less Christian), or of ideology (despite the Marxist associations of the ANC). It is a fundamental, basic clash between peoples differentiated solely by color, whose overriding grievance is the denial of their birthright and full participation in a country that is theirs, and their white rulers, who want to continue to retain their leading position (and their wealth, privileges, and way of life) in a country that is also theirs. Whites simply refuse to believe that the strong, rich country that they have run for so long (with African labor) can or will remain the same (for them) if Africans share or hold power. Thus prejudice is less the basis of the clash than is a fundamental rivalry for power, and for all that power means in the modern world.

The overriding issue that today separates Africans and whites is, in its starkest sense, political representation. Whites, especially those in government, are prepared now more than ever before to modify the exactions of apartheid in many ways providing that their own power is in no way eroded. Africans, who welcome increased economic opportunity, the freedom for the first time to form and join trade unions, and a modest provision of social services, insist that they will never be appeased for less than the franchise—and thus at least a meaningful portion of basic political power. They want what they have always wanted—basic human rights in a country that was theirs before the whites came, and in which they were systematically deprived of privileges and power by the might of whites.

Originally a microcosm of the South African situation, Namibia now is a separate but synergistically related zone of conflict, where the issues are stark, the solutions largely obvious and widely accepted, and success tantalizingly close at hand but still (and despite claims to the contrary) beyond easy grasp. As the previous chapter explained, despite many reasons that South Africa should want to withdraw from Namibia, there are compelling reasons that it has not. Thus the war for Namibia continues, with little sign that South Africa will soon vacate. It goes on despite South Africa's demonstrated ability to exert its will militarily in the region; despite the likelihood that South Africa's might and comparative economic weight could overawe any new government of a state as sparsely populated and economically weak as Namibia; and despite the fact that South Africa has no important financial, resource, or labor dependence upon Namibia.

Why? First, giving up Namibia could have adverse domestic political consequences for the National party that rules South Africa, but such a result is more and more discounted. Second, a withdrawal of South African troops might bring a Soviet-backed enemy that much closer to the heartland of the white-run regime. But the capital of Marxist Mozambique has always been located geographically much nearer to Pretoria and Johannesburg than Windhoek, Namibia's capital. Anyway, South Africa has proved itself militarily more decisive in the local context than was the Soviet Union. Third, South Africa wants to stay until a credible non-SWAPO local group is ready to receive power. That day will never come, however, and nearly all influential South Africans now realize that no combination of local interests and persons can conceivably appeal to the ultimate electorate more successfully than SWAPO. Moreover, as much as SWAPO operates with Soviet funds and arms, it cannot be asserted that a SWAPO-run Namibia could evade white South Africa's clutches any more than could the committed leadership of Mozambique.

These are all reasons for delay, but they are balanced or matched by arguments for a positive response. Two additional analyses are vital, if not decisive, in tipping the balance in favor of the status quo. First, for four years the immediate details as well as the overarching design of U.S. policy has rewarded South Africa and thus limited its incentives to depart. Second, without the leverage that control over Namibia gives South Africa in its long-standing tug of war with much of the remainder of the world, white rule would stand naked. Namibia is the prime bargaining counter for South Africa. So long as the United States and the West are engaged in the pursuit of Namibian independence, South Africa can afford to forestall Western attacks on apartheid itself and on the central nature of white power. Thus Namibia has diminished value for its own sake, but—particularly so long as Angola welcomes Cuban troops—enhanced worth for the long-run defense of white rule in South Africa.

A solution to the Namibian conflict is intimately related to and intertwined with the war in neighboring Angola. After Portugal relinquished control of its colony in 1975, three African groups competed for the right to succeed. Although the United States supported the Front for the National Liberation of Angola (FNLA) and to some extent backed the Union for the Total Independence of Angola (UNITA), Soviet and Cuban armed assistance to the Movement for the Popular Liberation of Angola (MPLA) proved decisive, especially after South Africa intervened on behalf of UNITA. Later the FNLA became moribund. UNITA, however, began working closely with South Africa and, by the late 1970s, posed a major threat to the MPLA's governance of the new country. In 1985, thanks to South Africa and to widespread support among southern Angolans, UNITA's military prowess threatens the hold of the MPLA government over at least three-fifths of Angola. In 1984 UNITA raiders attacked installations in the distant Cabinda enclave, captured foreigners working at the northern diamond mines, attacked a port city, and continued to cut the main railway line with impunity. Only the presence of 30,600 Cuban troops, resident in Angola since 1975, and the guidance of Soviet and East European advisers, deters an all-out battle for the whole of Angola.

The government of Angola believes itself militarily the equal of the forces of UNITA, but only with Cuban help. The United States has been urging Angola to send the Cubans home in exchange for U.S. recognition and economic aid. The Reagan administration has argued that once the Cubans go, South Africa can be persuaded to leave Namibia. After South Africa pulls back, it is assumed that logistical and air support for UNITA will wither, and a negotiated compromise or political coalition will be possible. Otherwise, Washington has argued, both wars will continue indefinitely, Angola will remain weak, the Soviets and the Cubans will reap their recompense in raw materials and coffee, and the possibilities of domestic growth will remain severely limited.

The Cubans, who last fought the South Africans seriously in 1975 and who now rarely engage UNITA, are officially Angola's bulwark as well as its albatross. Their presence provides a convenient excuse for South African intransigence over Namibia. The official U.S. acceptance of this position has also stymied the efforts of Washington to dampen or end hostilities in both countries. Indeed, U.S. policy for the region is buried beneath the rubble of failed attempts simultaneously to satisfy South Africa over the Cubans and the MPLA government over UNITA/

South Africa when every group (for SWAPO must also be included) naturally distrusts the intentions of others. There are other obvious flaws, too; for a Namibian settlement, and even a South African withdrawal from Namibia, need not guarantee or mandate a South African disengagement from or disavowal of UNITA. Even if it did, without the Cubans the MPLA might well be too weak to hold the guerrillas of UNITA at bay. There are too many imponderables, and too much at stake, for well-meant entreaties to prevail simply on their merits.

In 1984 there was a flurry of optimism when Mozambique, beleaguered by drought, ravaged by a cyclone, crippled by mismanagement, and severely harassed by a South African–prompted insurgency, signed a humbling peace and friendship treaty. Mozambique pledged to rid its terrain of the ANC, South Africa's prime guerrilla opponent. Despite Mozambique's friendship for the ANC and its abhorrence of apartheid, the former Portuguese colony was prepared to supplicate in order to obtain help. Most of all, South Africa promised Mozambique to cease supporting the MNR insurgent group. By March, when the Nkomati Accord was signed, the MNR was active in nine-tenths of Mozambique and had helped to cripple much of the poor country's economy. At about the same time, South Africa persuaded Angola to curb SWAPO in exchange for a withdrawal by South Africa from a 250-mile-long salient of territory that the whites had occupied (as part of their offensive against SWAPO) in 1981 and 1982.

In early 1985, optimism about South African intentions had faded. The MNR was still active in Mozambique. Economic targets remained vulnerable; the government of Mozambique had not yet begun to derive substantial benefits from its moral sacrifice at the beginning of the year. In Angola, claiming that the MPLA could not curb SWAPO, South Africa had still not returned its troops to Namibia. In February white soldiers still controlled over a twenty-five-mile-deep stretch of the southern section of the country. UNITA had stepped up its attacks on the MPLA-governed parts of Angola. Only in Zimbabwe had South Africa visibly moderated its backing for opponents of the nation's constituted government.

In terms of the elimination of intraregional conflict—a U.S. policy objective—there were some positive accomplishments during 1984. With the end of South African assistance, however limited, to the Ndebele rebels in southwestern Zimbabwe, the incipient civil war there was largely quelled. South Africa claimed to be ceasing its thoroughgoing involvement with the MNR. Botswana was peaceful. South Africa had not lately raided little Lesotho. Swaziland was calm, at least on the surface. South Africa had backed most of the way out of Angola. Most of all, certainly from the South African and probably from the U.S. official point of view,

Soviet influence in the region and on the conflicts of the region had been minimized, effectively by the Angolan–South African cease-fire and the signing of the Nkomati agreement between Mozambique and South Africa.

These recent accomplishments doubtless contribute to the peaceful evolution of southern Africa, and to that extent can be said to serve the aims in Africa of U.S. foreign policy. But the fundamental conflicts remain. In South Africa the urban riots of 1984 testified to the meaninglessness of white-imposed notions of reform for Africans. A death toll of 500 is but a fraction of the total in the Soweto riots of 1978, but it is 500 times greater than the deaths from incidents of urban unrest in the years since 1977. With a less particularized perspective, it is evident that the newly introduced South African constitution and its tricameral parliamentary configuration held no particular relevance for Africans. Nor were the still-to-be-imposed new urban arrangements advantageous for Africans. With the tightening of controls on unions, the harassment of the UDF, the detention of black leaders, and the government's disavowal of any desire radically to improve the political position of the majority, Africans had become as disenchanted as before with the practical workings as well as the philosophical underpinnings of apartheid. As far as they were concerned, nothing fundamental had changed. There were increased economic opportunities and broader social possibilities—but more so for the black elites and the middle class than for most Africans. Conceivably Africans will derive some political benefit from the participation of Asians and Coloureds in the new parliament, but most Africans (and most liberal whites) doubt that those groups will be able to play a meaningful legislative role in a parliament that is still dominated thoroughly by whites loyal to the National party. (The low polls in 1984 in the Coloured and Asian elections confirmed this disdain for the new, supposedly reformist, dispensation.)

The external aspect of this same conflict between black and white in South Africa still exists. Despite South Africa's successful assault on ANC basing privileges in Swaziland and Mozambique, and its equally skillful chilling of sanctuary possibilities for the ANC in Lesotho, Botswana, and Zimbabwe, guerrilla attacks show no diminution in quantity or quality. The ANC still survives to destroy fuel-storage tanks, government offices in several cities, critical strategic facilities, and so on. Moreover, in the eyes of the mass of blacks, the imprisoned leaders of the ANC are more popular now than in the 1960s and 1970s. According to several different respected opinion polls, Nelson Mandela and Walter Sisulu, the aging, originally militant leaders of the ANC, are the overwhelming favorites of the inhabitants of the black cities and townships. Everything that the white government of South Africa has done to combat the ANC since

1976 has instead enhanced its status, and given Mandela and Sisulu the glory of folk heroes.

Beyond South Africa's borders the positive accomplishments of recent months still leave smoldering wars in Angola, Namibia, and Mozambique. The scale of the conflict in Mozambique may lessen by the end of this year, but the battles for the other two locales are certain to continue at their present levels, if not intensify, during late 1984 and 1985.

At the core of all these rivalries, even that of Angola, is the persistence of apartheid. Moreover, the only standing that the Soviets still have in the region is as an opponent of white domination. They lack credibility as a donor or investor, but they do give funds and arms to liberation movements. If the United States is concerned about the Soviet and Cuban threat to stability in southern Africa, and the links that such a threat must continue to have to larger, global antagonisms between East and West, then apartheid is the prime obstacle to a significant reduction in East-West tensions in much of Africa.

The strategic aims of U.S. policy, despite some tactical changes, are nearly the same at mid-decade as they were in late 1980, before the presidential election of that year. In other words, very little of a positive nature has been achieved during the period through 1984. Indeed, from critical South African perspectives, the years from 1980 to 1984 distinctly set back the region and black interests in South Africa. White South Africa is more powerful locally and regionally than it was in 1980, its might unchallenged in a way that was unthinkable in 1980. Yet the economic and social conditions of its neighbors, as well as the economic, social, and political conditions of its internal black majority, are more immiserated than they were in 1980. Economic mismanagement in the black countries, climatic misfortune, and the sad world currents of economic reverse have all played crucial roles in the neighborhood; but so have the economic and military assaults of South Africa. Within that country, too, the performance of indicators of black economic growth have been spotty. Certainly life in the homelands, where there is abundant malnutrition and overcrowding, is demonstrably poorer. So, too, is it in many cities and towns, where housing and other social services have been curtailed, squatters attacked, and the noose of apartheid tightened. Nor can apologists show solid evidence of new political opportunities in South Africa for Africans. The crux of all debates is political participation; and in that fundamental, as in so many other aspects of apartheid, nothing has changed since 1980. Many categories of complaint can be termed more damaging. As the simple goal enunciated in Vienna in 1977 by Vice-President Mondale remains unmet, so must conflict deepen in South Africa and episodes of violence cascade upon the people of that land. South Africa's apartheid remains a charge on the conscience as well as the self-interest of the West.

The Carter administration sought to curtail conflict in southern Africa and accelerate the abolition of apartheid by castigating and isolating South Africa. It fulminated in private and public. It threatened the imposition of unspecified sanctions. It shunned trade, embargoed commodities, minimized investments, and limited lending. Occasionally, it rewarded good efforts. It had a goal: progress toward full political participation by all South Africans regardless of color. It suggested a means: consultation and negotiation between blacks and whites—something along the lines of a constitutional congress. Despite the famous Mondale slip in Vienna, however, it never demanded one man, one vote, now.

The Carter administration can claim several achievements. It compelled South Africa to reverse a long-held position and admit that Namibia was, in fact, an international responsibility and was not, either de facto or de jure, a part of South Africa. It persuaded the South Africans to begin a process of negotiation over Namibia's future that, even if it still limps along, has already resulted in a series of agreements that could someday lead to an internationally validated establishment of independence.

Harder to demonstrate is the impact of the policies of the Carter administration on internal improvements in South Africa. The significant labor reforms that were begun then owe at least some impetus to Western criticism. One perceptive South African commentator claims that there is no doubt "that the threat of sanctions, boycotts and disinvestment played a role in deciding Pretoria to give trade union rights to blacks."[1]

Western carping also encouraged the discussions, however flawed in their ultimate execution, that led to the construction of a new parliament that now includes representatives of dark-pigmented people. Perhaps the Carter policies encouraged the razing of fewer rather than more squatter camps and limited removals. Perhaps South Africa deferred the destabilization of its neighbors until President Carter lost the election of 1980. Or perhaps the timing of much of the military action against South Africa's neighbors reflected changes in official thinking and military tactics that were unconnected with the shift in U.S. policy.

Whatever the etiology of South African resurgence in the 1980s, there is no doubt that in 1985 its armed forces are stronger and bolder than they were in 1980. None can dispute their willingness to attack and successfully overawe their neighbors by one after another audacious raid. Indeed, in 1983–1984, they faced down the Soviets—and won. Toward the end of the Carter years, South Africa did raid SWAPO bases in Angola. But the wholesale adoption of this tactic, and the occupation of large swaths of territory, occurred during the Reagan administration's watch. So did air attacks on Maputo and Maseru, the subversion of Swaziland, and the promotion of a wholly concocted insurgency movement in nearby Mozambique.

South Africa tried in the 1980s to give Swaziland large chunks of homeland South Africa. Near its internal homelands it relocated, removed, and shifted nearly a million Africans with impunity. It sharply reduced the number of persons banned, but continued (especially in late 1984) to detail and interrogate Africans for long periods without charges or trials. South African critics of their government have claimed that human rights and civil liberties for blacks have deteriorated severely during the Reagan years. At a bare minimum, the policy of constructive engagement—introduced with fanfare in 1981 as a break with the Carter administration's antagonism—brought little discernible improvement to the daily life of blacks in South Africa. The main cruelties of the apartheid system—the enforced removal of Africans from so-called white areas; the relentless inferiority of black education, health, and housing; and the security laws that give police virtually unlimited powers to enforce racial codes—all remain intact.[2]

Constructive engagement was designed to do what it has not—to deliver Namibia, end globally connected and South African–inspired conflict in the region, and start South Africa down the evolutionary road toward fuller political participation for all. Constructive engagement emphasizes friendship and relaxed dealings with white South Africa. As a result, and despite the Reagan administration's reiterated abhorrence of apartheid, U.S. relations with South Africa since 1980 have been much more amicable than at any time since 1960. This closeness was intended to produce positive results.

Chester Crocker, assistant secretary of state for Africa and the architect of constructive engagement, summarized his personal approach in an interview with a South African magazine editor. He was asked how he perceived the relationship in 1984 between the United States and South Africa, "especially in view of past posturing?" Crocker replied:

> One develops personal familiarity with key decision-makers which pays dividends. We hope that we have achieved that with South Africa and with other key countries in the region. It's a two way street—a matter of developing a track record. Undoubtedly one can over time do business more effectively when one knows the people at the table, where they are coming from, and how they tend to think and operate. We take the South African Government as an important and serious partner. We share certain goals. We see clearly where we don't agree. The past few years have been a learning process. I believe each government takes the other seriously—which has not always been the case.[3]

Crocker persistently rejected claims that white control of South Africa has been strengthened during his time in office. "The dynamic we see," he told *The Guardian,* "is one of growing debate, open discussion and ferment in the white community, but also among the coloureds and Asians." He said that the South African government "has decided to test its own power base" by broadening the nature of its parliamentary representation. He believed that the Nkomati Accord dealt "a body blow" to the illusion that armed struggle would solve South Africa's problems. The Nkomati agreement was important because it endorsed sovereignty for South Africa's neighbors as well as itself, and showed the importance of statehood and survival. It also presaged economic cooperation. On Namibia, Crocker blamed the Cubans for the failure to achieve independence. This was the rock on which constructive engagement had truly foundered. But, Crocker explained: "there has to be something in it for everybody, including the party which controls Namibia today. There is no doubt in our minds that the South Africans would like to see a settlement in Namibia sooner rather than later."[4]

To engage South Africa constructively was less venal than naive. The South Africans, confident of the power of their Namibian hand, simply dangled the specter of cooperation before inexperienced game theorists who had foresworn sanctions (and therefore the employment of effective sticks). Crocker and his associates were left with carrots, each and all of which the South Africans were pleased to consume. The United States relaxed its commercial embargo, reaffirmed intelligence links, cooperated in the nuclear field, moderated public criticism at home and abroad, and affirmed closer relations in and with South Africa. But the biggest carrot of all was the Cuban issue. To have made the Cubans hostage for Namibia reversed the entire drift of negotiations, permitted South Africa to relax, and has delayed independence indefinitely. For no Angolan government could easily throw itself on the mercy of the West (and South Africa) when UNITA remained a clear and present danger.

Crocker and his associates may still think that they can square the unholy triangle, but to believe so is optimistic. The United States has made dozens of concessions. South Africa has been rewarded. But there has been no attempt at operant conditioning: South Africa has feared no little punishment. Indeed, the basic flaw in constructive engagement was and is its lack of an incentive structure. The concessions were made willy nilly, in no hierarchical sequence that might have commanded South African attention, if not positive performances.

What next? It *is* in the self-interest of a U.S. government that wants to minimize conflict in southern Africa, negate the influence of the Soviet Union in that region, and encourage conditions there favorable to rising standards of living and broader political participation (not to mention justice, equity, and human rights), to devise a new policy that will achieve short- and long-term results without instantly forfeiting an ability to influence trends as they develop. We *do* want evolution rather than revolution to be South Africa's fate, providing that the evolution is progressive and that it commences soon and proceeds at a more than deliberate pace. We want South Africa to remain prosperous, but in shared hands. We want South Africa to continue producing its minerals and crops, and to play a greater and more responsible role in the politics and economics of Africa.

The test of a new policy will be its ability to concentrate the mind of official South Africa—to pull or push the oligarchical state to think anew about its real options in the world, in the region, and at home. By rewarding positive trends and withholding rewards or ensuring at least verbal unpleasantness for negative departures, South Africa could again begin to appreciate the real risks of acts and policies deplored by the West. Since 1980 South Africa has borne almost no cost, suffered no shame and obloquy, and (among whites at home) accelerated from strength to strength. There are sanctions that can be threatened, mostly in the field of communications and transport. If necessary, at minimal cost to the United States, those threats could be made real. Continued lending and investment could be subject to progress along defined paths, as Senator Paul Tsongas once proposed. Boycotts of various kinds are possible. But it is the aggregate of pressure that matters. It will prove influential only when the leaders of white South Africa count the cost too high and agree to sit down to talk with the true leaders of the black community. The point is not to hit out blindly at South Africa but to devise a carefully calibrated series of incentives which that country could reasonably be expected to seek and which would bring about the major policy shifts that black leaders in South Africa, many whites, and many foreigners so patently desire.

The United States can, in exchange for its continued friendship, the possibility of broadened trade relations, and increased investments, expect the cessation of destabilization, a swift finalizing of the independence arrangements for Namibia, and a beginning to the long and arduous process of negotiating new internal political institutions and arrangements with representatives of the majority. It can encourage the gradual decay of apartheid and the slow but necessary integration of Africans into the fabric of what is now a powerful, privileged white society. These overdue utopian steps will be wrenching and painful, and they will take time. The United States has a role not as an arbitrator but as a catalyst and, if absolutely necessary, as a facilitator. Since any reorientation of policy, U.S. or South African, will take time and patience, there are a few interim postures that ought to be struck, both by official Americans in South Africa and by the United States with regard to the South African question more generally. We should search for the pressure points of the white society, and make it known that we *do* intend to push hard—but fairly—on those very spots. We ought to offer more vocal public and private criticism of South African misconceptions and missteps. Not only for moral but also for bargaining reasons we should have expressed our outrage at the attempt to give KaNgwane and Ingwavumaland to Swaziland. We missed an opportunity at Dreifontein, after Saul Mkhize's death, to put white South Africa on the metaphorical rack. We can specify particular goals in the labor and industrial fields, quietly if necessary, but firmly. We can help find funds for black schooling. We need publicly to resume contacts with black opponents of the white government, affirmations of friendship that have subtly been permitted to wither during the Reagan years. In other words, we need to take black politics seriously, an omission of recent times. We can talk to the ANC, abroad. We can fruitfully employ the multinational, Contact Group formula to give even more weight to any determined approach to South Africa.

Is this an efficacious formula? Certainly, at least in theory. Its flaw is its pollyannish quality, but its virtue is in stressing the obvious. Certainly a policy of carrots without sticks has been shown to be unworkable and foolish. A policy of sticks alone will, by definition, achieve nothing. There is a middle way; but whether the vicissitudes of real time and real events will permit an incentive-based, hierarchically structured, simple psychological model to achieve results in the complex environment of white-dominated South Africa is more a hope than a promise. However, such a shift is imperative if our own foreign-policy needs are to be achieved, and progress is to be attempted in the modernizing of South Africa.

Notes

1. Alister Sparks, *The Star Weekly,* 30 July 1984.
2. Glenn Frankel, "Debate Rends Facade of Apartheid's Executors," *The Washington Post,* 29 July 1984.
3. Interview between Hugh Murray and Chester Crocker, "Crocker," *Leadership SA,* III, 2 (1984), 41.
4. Crocker, quoted in *The Guardian,* 20 July 1984.

Index

South Africa and *Southern Africa* are not indexed separately.

Salisbury (Harare), Rhodesia (Zimbabwe), 33

San (Bushmen), people of Namibia, 138

Saõ Tomé and Príncipe, 55, 57

Sardines, 139

Sasol, oil-from-coal plant, South Africa, 22

SAT (South African Transport Services), 114, 118, 126

Saudi Arabia, 30

Savimbi, Jonas, leader of UNITA, 4, 83

Schlebusch Commission, South Africa, 22

Security Council of the United Nations, 45

Security Council Resolution 435, 37, 65, 141, 142, 143

Security, Intelligence and State Security Council Act, #64, 16–17

Selassie, Haile, emperor of Ethiopia, 57

Senegal, 32

Sensitivity dependence, 115–116

Seychelles, 24, 39, 57, 59, 91

Shaba Province, Zaire, 56

Sheep, 139

Shipanga, Andreas, leader of SWAPO-D, 142

Sisulu, Walter, leader of ANC, 157, 158

Smith, Ian, prime minister of Rhodesia, 36; rebellion, 77, 84

Sobhuza II, king of Swaziland, 5, 6

Soil conservation, 93

Somalia, 33, 39, 56, 58, 91

Sorghum, 137

Sotho, people of Lesotho, 112, 116

South African Communist Party. *See* SACP

South African Council of Churches, 41

South African Institute of International Affairs (Johannesburg), 10

South African Transport Services. *See* SAT

South West Africa People's Organization. *See* SWAPO

South West African National Union. *See* SWANU

Southern African Customs Union. *See* SACU

Southern African Development Bank, 105, 110

Southern African Development Coordinating Conference. *See* SADCC

Southern African Labour Commission. *See* SALC

Southern African Regional Tourist Council (SARTOC), 98

Soviet Union, 2, 3, 4, 5, 7, 9, 10, 11, 17, 81, 83, 139, 140, 148, 151, 153, 155, 158, 161; foreign policy, 27–30; policy in Africa south of the Sahara, 30–34; policy in southern Africa, 34–40; policy toward South Africa, 40–50

Soweto, South Africa: riots, 4, 9, 56, 65, 157

Soweto Civic Association, South Africa, 153

Sputnik, 31

SSC (State Security Council), South Africa, 4, 13–14, 17, 18–21, 22, 23, 24, 25

START (Strategic Arms Reduction Talks), 46

State Security Council. *See* SSC

Steel, 126

Steyn Commission, South Africa, 22

Strategic Arms Reduction Talks. *See* START

Sub-Saharan Africa, 37

Sudan, 55, 151

Swakopmund, Namibia, 138

SWANU (South West African National Union), 142

SWAPO (South West Africa People's Organization), 2, 4, 5, 6, 7, 9, 34, 37, 45, 47, 56, 59, 60, 62, 64, 65, 67, 83, 85, 123, 139–42, 156, 159

SWAPO-D (SWAPO Democrats), 142

Swaziland, 5, 6, 24, 61, 62, 71, 72, 73, 77, 91, 93, 96, 98, 99, 109,

About the Authors

Robert I. Rotberg is professor of political science and history at the Massachusetts Institute of Technology. He previously taught at Harvard University. He edits the *Journal of Interdisciplinary History,* is a trustee of the World Peace Foundation and of Oberlin College, and writes regularly for the *Christian Science Monitor* and other newspapers. Among his many books on African and Caribbean politics, the most recent are *Suffer the Future: Policy Choices in Southern Africa* (Harvard University Press, 1980); *Conflict and Compromise in South Africa* (Lexington Books, 1980), with John Barratt; *Namibia: Political and Economic Prospects* (Lexington Books, 1983); and *Imperialism, Colonialism, and Hunger: East and Central Africa* (Lexington Books, 1983).

Henry S. Bienen is director of the Center for International Studies and is the James S. McDonnell Distinguished University Professor in the Woodrow Wilson School of Public and International Affairs, Princeton University. He edits *World Politics* and is a member of the Council on Foreign Relations. Among his many books are *Kenya: The Politics of Participation and Control* (Princeton University Press, 1974); *Armies and Parties in Africa* (Holmes & Meier, 1978); and *Nigeria: Absorbing the Oil Wealth* (International Publishers, 1982).

Robert Legvold is associate director of the W. Averell Harriman Institute for Advanced Study of the Soviet Union and professor of political science at Columbia University. He was a senior fellow at the Council on Foreign Relations and formerly taught at Tufts University. He is the author of *Soviet Policy in West Africa* (Harvard University Press, 1970).

Gavin S. Maasdorp is the director of the Economic Research Unit and professor of economics at the University of Natal. He is a member of the executive council of the South African Institute of International Affairs, and has extensive experience as a transportation consultant in Swaziland. He is the author of *SADCC: A Post-Nkomati Evaluation* (South African Institute of International Affairs, 1984).